MORRIS & CHAN
ON
FLY FISHING TROUT LAKES

Skip Morris & Brian Chan

Frank
Amato
PORTLAND

Dedications

I dedicate this book to the two men who in four years taught me more about trout lakes than I had learned in all the previous decades: Brian Chan and Gordon Honey.

—Skip Morris

Dedicated to: Janine and C.W. (Carlyn) Chan who understand my passion for fishing.

—Brian Chan

Acknowledgments

Brian and I wish to thank each of the following people who helped us create *Morris & Chan on Fly Fishing Trout Lakes* **by providing information, photographs, or access to lakes:**

In particular, guide Gordon Honey for sharing his vast knowledge of the lakes of the Kamloops Region, Carol Ann Morris for the many hours she dedicated to getting the photographs and illustrations just right (and for partially laying out this book), and Rick Hafele for his invaluable help with aquatic insects.

Additionally: Derick MacDonald of Lac Le Jeune Resort, Bruce Harpole and the Oregon Fishing Club, Roger Hudspeth (owner and manager of Barnes Butte Lake, Oregon), Dave Gunderson, Douglas Lake Ranch (British Columbia, Canada), Bill and Doreen Nelson, Bill Schiess, Stan Horton of Staley Springs Lodge (on Henrys Lake, Idaho), Jim Wheeler of Spring Creek Prams, Ted Leeson, Jack Ohman, Jim Schollmeyer, Dave Hughes, Andy Burk, Brian O'Keefe, Ken Strand, Mike Seim, Arnie Koch, Teddy and Brice Tedford, Ron Boudreau, Pat Kendall, Steve Lemieux, Russ Crocker, Canadian Peter Morrison #1 of Springbrook Manufacturing, Canadian Peter Morrison #2 and Bill Demchuk of Osprey Fly Fishing Adventures, Eagle Electronics, The Wood River Co., Dean Kelley and the Port Ludlow Marina, Frosty Foust, and Debbie Honey.

Conversion Table

Linear Measure
1/8 inch = 0.3175 centimeters = 3.175 millimeters
4 inches = 10.16 centimeters
12 inches = 1 foot = 30.48 centimeters
20 feet = 6.096 meters
1 yard = 0.9144 meters
1 mile = 1,609.35 meters = 1.61 kilometers

Weight
1 pound = 0.454 kilograms = 454 grams
5 pounds = 2.27 kilograms = 2,270 grams

Temperature
Fahrenheit to Centigrade: $F-32^0 \times 0.555 = C$
$50^0 F = 9.99^0 (10^0, \text{ really}) C$
$65^0 F = 18.32^0 C$

Published in 1999 by:
Frank Amato Publications, Inc.
PO Box 82112 • Portland, Oregon 97282
(503) 653-8108

Softbound UPC: 0-66066-00392-8   Softbound ISBN-13: 978-1-57188-181-6
Hardbound UPC: 0-66066-00393-5   Hardbound ISBN-10 : 1-57188-182-4

All photographs taken by Carol Morris unless otherwise noted.
Cover photo: Brian O'Keefe
Frontispiece: Ken Scheer
Back cover photo and inset of Skip Morris: Carol Morris
Back cover inset of Brian Chan: Lloyd Horwood

Illustrations: Carol Morris

Design conception: Carol Morris
Layout: Tony Amato

Printed in Hong Kong

3 4 5 6 7 8 9 10

Contents

A BEGINNING

The abundance of information in this book will be a real godsend if you're ready for it. But if you're new to fishing trout lakes, you could find so much detail overwhelming, no matter how well it's organized or how clearly it's presented. So if your experience as a lake fisher is slim or nonexistent, this short chapter is for you—it will soon get you out fishing trout lakes simply and effectively.

There is another chapter—Chapter 13, "First Lake, New Lake," beginning on page 83—that will be a great help to you if you're new to lakes. It prepares you for your first day on a trout lake, then, step by simple step, guides you through that day. But even that chapter sometimes assumes that you have at least some lake-fishing experience. This chapter does not.

If you're not only new to lakes but new to *fly fishing* altogether, then you need to start with a true beginner's fly-fishing book. It will teach you how to rig a rod, how to tie a fly onto your tippet, a few other essential but straightforward operations, and about the standard terminology of the sport. That's really not so much to learn, but it's enough to carry out the bare-bones, first-day-of-lake-fishing plan that follows.

EQUIPMENT

To fish at all effectively on the majority of trout lakes, you'll need some kind of watercraft. Chapter 10, "Boats, Float Tubes, and Tackle" (beginning on page 68) will help you select one and the components it requires—oars or fins, waders, and such. But you may be able to rent; fly shops and lakeside resorts often rent boats and float tubes. Or perhaps you can borrow one from a friend.

Chapter 10 also lists a basic selection of tackle (rod, reel, lines, and other such items), which you'll also need. You'll find two short, very basic lists of lake flies for starting out—one list for the fly tier, another for the purchaser—in Chapter 8 under the heading "A Beginning Selection of Flies" on page 60.

TECHNIQUE

The easiest way to fish your first trout lake is to "troll," essentially, towing a fly behind a long line. Trolling is described on pages 18 and 19 in Chapter 3, "Fishing the Depths." It's an effective method. Troll with a type III full-sinking line, a 9-foot 3X tapered leader, and two feet of 4X tippet. (For details on leaders and tippet, see "Leader" on page 74. Also, see Chapter 11, "Knots," beginning on page 79.) Use a fly of fair size—a size-8 Black, Brown, or Olive Woolly Bugger would be good, as would a Peacock Chenille Leech or a Skip's Furry Dragon. Experiment with the speed of your watercraft, the location, depth, and the amount of line you have out. If all this fails to bring a strike after a half hour or so (with occasional checks of the fly for debris), try trolling something smaller, a size-12 Halfback or Skip Nymph or the like. Keep experimenting until you get a strike. Or take a break, to give the fish some time to decide they're hungry.

Take advantage of how trolling allows you to look around. Scan the water and shallows and shoreline and even the sky. Observe and learn.

If trout are feeding at the surface, or begin to after you've begun trolling deep, you can rig up a full-floating line with a 9-foot 4X tapered leader and three feet of 5X tippet and troll the surface with a size-12 or -14 nymph, such as a Skip Nymph or Gold Ribbed Hare's Ear. Or, by dressing your leader and tippet and a size-12 Tom Thumb with fly floatant, you can troll a dry fly. But only troll with a floating line if the trout are showing at the surface in at least fair numbers—deep trolling with a full-sinking line is the most reliable approach.

Troll slowly, and when in doubt, troll *more* slowly.

WHEN

Time of year and time of day will strongly influence your chances of catching trout. "The Seasons," on pages 39 and 40 in Chapter 6, "The Life of a Trout Lake," will help you decide when to try fishing your first lake. And you can only improve your odds for success by reading two other topics in Chapter 6: "Temperature," on page 38 (under "Trout Survival") and "Weather" on page 40.

WHERE TO FISH IN A LAKE

Begin trolling in water about 15 to 20 feet deep (unless, of course, you're trolling with a full-floating line, in which case you should troll wherever the trout are showing). Troll roughly parallel with the shoreline but, as always, experiment.

As to where you'll likely find trout, see Chapter 5, "Reading a Lake," which begins on page 30—it's short, but clear and helpful.

WHAT NEXT?

When you've spent enough time trolling that you're ready to try something new, read Chapter 13, "First Lake, New Lake" (which I described on the previous page—it'll be a big help no matter what approach you try next). If you can make casts of about 45 feet, you might try dropping anchor and working your nymph close to the bottom on a type I or type II full-sinking line by counting down, as described on page 15 in Chapter 3, "Fishing the Depths." You could even try floating-line, deep-fly fishing, which is also described in Chapter 3 on pages 16 and 17. Or, if trout are rising well, you could work those rises as described in Chapter 4, "Fishing the Surface Layer", which begins on page 20.

Beyond that, read and then reread the whole of this book, be always open-minded, experiment, and learn.

GENERAL TECHNIQUES FOR FISHING TROUT LAKES

T hese are the elemental moves and strategies for fishing a trout lake. They are simple enough and easily absorbed and will soon be fixed. You'll wonder then how anyone could fish a trout lake without them.

THE HAND-TWIST RETRIEVE

The single best thing about the hand-twist retrieve is that the angler keeps a sound grip on the line throughout—trout seem always to strike when the angler is unprepared. The strip retrieve so many fly fishers instinctively use has vulnerable moments built in; the hand-twist retrieve does not.

The hand-twist retrieve also tends to cure a problem all novice lake fishers share—they work most flies too quickly. But while the hand is learning, the fly swims at an insect's pace, instead of speeding like a frightened fish. In time the muscles find their rhythm, and then this retrieve can be quick, for those rare times when it should be.

1. Instructions here are for right-handers. Partly uncurl the first finger of your right hand (the hand that is holding the rod) and lightly drape the line across it. Bring your thumb down to your finger to contain the line.

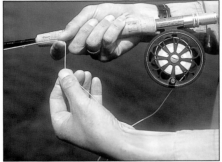

2. Grasp the line lightly between your *left-hand* first finger and thumb, just below your right hand. Rotate your forearm and bend your wrist to draw in a bit of line, the line sliding across your right-hand first finger.

3. With your *left-hand* rotated to palm-up, catch the line lightly with the little finger of that hand.

4. Return your hand to its former position by bending your wrist and, again, rotating your forearm. This motion, too, draws in some line.

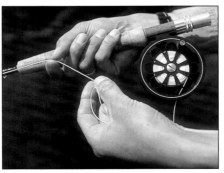

5. Now catch the line again with your first finger and thumb. This completes a full hand-twist. In time you'll perform them in smooth succession.

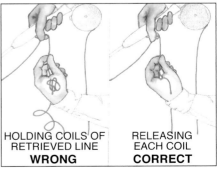

HOLDING COILS OF RETRIEVED LINE
WRONG

RELEASING EACH COIL
CORRECT

6. The hand-twist retrieve fills the hand with coils of line. Try to drop them often, so the weight of the hanging line can stretch them straight.

STRIP RETRIEVE

The strip retrieve is natural, simple. But unlike the hand-twist retrieve it has inherent weak moments, which come as control of the line is passed from hand to hand. Reserve the strip retrieve for the quick-swimming fly and for long smooth swims connected by pauses—but because both are rarely appropriate, prefer the hand-twist retrieve.

1. Instructions here are for right-handers. Hold the rod in your right hand and the line in your right-hand first finger and thumb. (If you're left-handed turn these instructions around.) With your left hand, grasp the line near the right hand; then loosen your grip on the line with your right as you draw the line down with your left. This is "stripping" line, and the strips can be slow to fast, short to long.

2. At the end of the draw, release the line with your left hand as you tighten on it with your right. Raise your left hand up to your right hand, grasp the line, and strip it again. Soon you'll be able to make rapid strips so the fly zips along, though it's questionable whether you should.

THE DIRECT CONNECTION FROM FLY TO HAND

Watch an experienced fly fisher work a fly on a sinking line. Curiously, his rod-tip will be angled sharply down, touching or even piercing the water's surface. This is neither laziness nor severe weakness of the wrist; the point is to keep the line and leader as straight as possible—a direct connection from fly to hand. Never will this straightness be perfect, but the fewer the waves and bends, the more firmly and immediately the angler will feel a touch of the fly.

A rod-tip raised creates a belly in the line, slack, a dampener against the fly communicating to the hand. Always with a sinking line, sometimes even with a floating line, the rod-tip should be lowered to the water so the angler can extend his touch out to the fly.

THE RAISED ROD-TIP—AN ERROR

ROD-TIP TO WATER—CORRECT

Here is the proper pose of the lake fisher fishing with a sinking line (and sometimes with a floating line, as described later in this chapter under "Striking")—the dropped rod, its tip to the water, rod and line roughly aligned from all viewpoints.

STRAIGHT LINE, STRAIGHT LEADER

Consider this another facet of the previous topic—"The Direct Connection From Fly to Hand." Kinks and coils in leader or line dampen that critical connection between the angler and his fly—no angler's touch is so keen that he can feel a tug at the fly through a leader spiraled like a soft spring. Additionally, on a shooting cast, line-coils may bunch and tangle into a variety of challenging puzzles.

Straighten a leader, new or old, by stretching it tightly between the hands, working from end to end. Do the same with lines that coil or tangle. To reduce the curling of line and leader, wind them only lightly onto the reel, especially if you are putting that reel aside overnight or until the next fishing trip.

Here is the result of not stretching a fly line: a stunning display of macramé art.

A fly line can also tangle because it is twisted, which usually is caused by a fly that believes it's a propeller. First, cut off the fly; second, cast and then feed out the full length of the line behind your boat or tube; third, tow the line briefly (it should now be free of twist); fourth, tie on a new fly or figure out how to fix the old fly (or rightfully destroy the accursed thing).

THE LEVER RETRIEVE

Few good lake anglers regularly use this approach, and it's generally considered faulty. I use it fairly often. It goes on the theory that the angled rod is a lever, so any resistance at its tip is magnified in the hand. For me it works, but it is unconventional, and Brian scowls when he sees me use it.

But there are times—and plenty of them—when the lever retrieve just makes sense. Sometimes it is really the only choice: The wind, or perhaps the current from a feeder stream, has swung the line around to where the rod can't follow; the other angler in the boat has positioned his rod where yours should be; your float tube or boat has drifted to where pointing your rod directly at your line is awkward. All these situations demand the lever retrieve, and there are others that will demand it, too.

With the rod-tip touching the water and the rod at an angle to the line (the exact angle is a matter of personal preference) the rod acts as a lever. It amplifies the line's resistance in the hand—a touch to the fly is clearly and instantly felt. (That, at least, is the theory.) A rod that is particularly heavy or supple, of course, will dampen the signals from the fly.

STRIKING

It's often called a "strike" when a fish takes a fly, but it's also called a "strike" when the angler pulls the line to set the hook in a fish that's taken a fly. The fish *strikes*, the angler *strikes*—confusing. Somehow, though, these meanings are seldom confused by anglers, even when unexpected action sets them to shouting, "You've got a strike!" "Strike or you'll lose him!" "Finally— someone got a strike!" "Don't strike too hard!" and such.

With a sinking line, or with any unseen take of the fly, immediately set the hook upon feeling the fish. This hook-set, or "strike," is just a light quick raising of the rod-tip, which tugs the hook point in. The line-hand firmly holds the line but must be set to feed it out when the fish begins to run. The lighter the tippet, the lighter the strike, but always quick and immediate with an invisible take.

With a dry fly, simply strike when you see the trout take—don't wait to feel it. If you are missing fish, strike slightly later, a half-second pause between signal and response. When casting to rising fish with a nymph (or with any fly that is sunk), do not strike by sight. Keep the rod-tip low and strike only when you feel the take. Striking to the sight of a boil is usually striking too soon.

PLAYING A TROUT

The bottom line with playing any trout is to keep it out of trouble until it's tired enough to net. In lakes, there's usually so much open water that the angler has the advantage and the trout has little trouble available to get himself into. But it's not always so easy.

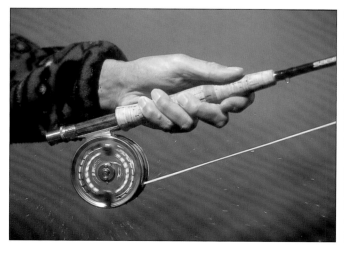

When a trout is first hooked, he will usually make a long run or two. Keep the reel's drag low enough to let him go, to give line instead of snapping the leader. I prefer my drags set quite low, so I can lightly grasp the emerging line and adjust resistance on it (or palm the reel's spool, if the reel is designed for that). Later in the battle he may choose to run again. Let him. And enjoy.

Throughout the fight, keep your rod tipped up so that its flex can help protect the leader. But don't exaggerate the angle, or your rod, not your leader, will be at risk— 45^0 between the rod's butt section and the water's surface is a good standard.

Mostly, play a trout on a tight line, constant firm pressure. Too many hooks pulling free in battle probably means too light a touch. But when a hooked trout leaps, *lighten* your strain on the line. In the air he's free to slap his tail against the leader which, if tight, may part.

Obviously it's possible to press a trout too hard—snap the leader or tear the hook free. And, of course, if he wants to really run, let him. Still, a tight line brings the best results. Playing trout is like everything else about fishing for them—a guessing game heavily dependent upon luck.

If the trout is clearly on his way to trouble—an anchor line, brush, water plants, a dock—drop the rod-tip to slacken the line and the trout may halt its run, convinced he's free. This doesn't always work, but it's always worth a try when no other options remain.

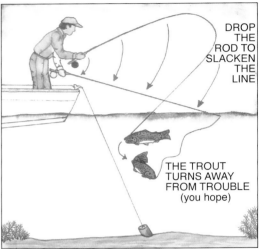

DROP THE ROD TO SLACKEN THE LINE

THE TROUT TURNS AWAY FROM TROUBLE (you hope)

THE SLACK-LINE STRATEGY

NETTING AND RELEASING

Scooping a trout up in a net may seem an obvious move, but it's not. It's not a difficult move either, but it helps a great deal to know the right way.

1. When the trout is ready (tired and manageable but not exhausted—truly exhausted trout may not survive), dip the rim of the net into the water and slide the trout in, head up, head first.

2. When the bulk of the trout is past the rim, raise the net.

3. Keep the trout in the water as much as possible. Never squeeze the trout, as doing so could crush its organs. Instead, cradle it in hands and fingers that, though rigid, apply no pressure.

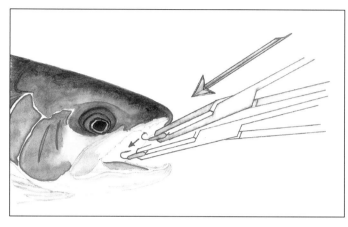

4. Clamp the fly in forceps, then back it out opposite the direction of penetration. (There are other hook-removing tools besides forceps. See "Hook Remover" in Chapter 10, "Boats, Float Tubes, and Tackle," page 75.)

5. Gently cradle the trout—*keeping its head fully submerged so that it can breathe*. Remember: holding a trout's head up in the air is like holding *your* head under water. Let the trout leave your hands only when it does so on its own. Big trout often take longer to revive than small trout.

ANCHORING

A loosely patterned search, such as wind drifting, trolling, and working a shoreline, can be very effective and the wisest way to fish for scattered trout. Other times the angler's position should be fixed—as with the floating line and deep chironomid pupa or when the trout are grouped and feeding at the surface because the insects they have found are gathered on a patch of water. Whenever the fixed position is called for, the angler in a float tube or boat must anchor.

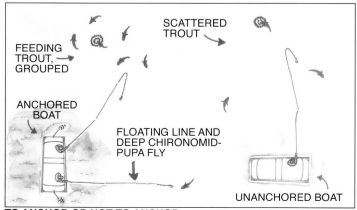

TO ANCHOR OR NOT TO ANCHOR

By paying out plenty of line you make your anchor more effective than by tethering it tight. The long line is best in brisk wind. A really powerful wind will probably root up any anchor, but in such a wind you probably should be safely ashore anyway.

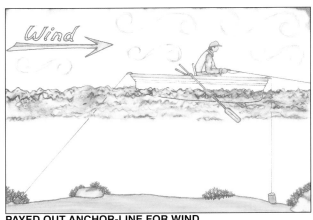

PAYED OUT ANCHOR-LINE FOR WIND

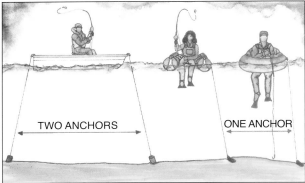

TWO ANCHORS   ONE ANCHOR

ANCHORING BOATS AND FLOAT TUBES

A two-anchor setup really is required in a boat for fine control of the fly. Lower first the anchor at the bow, belay its line, and then lower the anchor at the stern. Brian and I have never felt the need for more than one anchor in float tubes and kick-boats.

TWO ANGLERS, ONE BOAT

When two fly fishers share a single boat, as often they do, it may be efficient and pleasant or it may be hell. Here's how to avoid fishing the River Styx:

1. Since both fly fishers usually want to cast off the same side of the boat, try to find a left-handed partner if you are a right, a right-handed partner if you are a left. Then cast slightly side-arm.
2. If the boat is small, or you both cast with the same arm, try to get as far apart as possible. This often means piling the gear in the center of the boat, between you.
3. Just before you cast, call out, "Casting" or something similar. If your partner calls out and you are already casting—especially if you are casting at a different angle than he is—inform him of the potential problem: "Oh my *God—nooooo!*" is popular. What's great about this system is that you can each cast at whatever angles you please (so long as your casts don't put a hook into your partner; see "Glasses" in Chapter 10, page 76). This system has made two in a boat a much smoother operation for me, all other considerations

Two anglers casting from a single boat in harmony. Parallel casting, as here, is one solution. As described above, there are others.

WORKING A SMALL AREA

Often there is a little sphere or strip of water that holds special promise. In all but flat-calm conditions, cleanly and thoroughly working such areas, especially from a boat, will probably call for anchoring. The float-tube fisherman may be able to hold his place comfortably without an anchor, or he may not. The point is, with either floating line or sinking, fishing the surface or well down, if you are going to effectively fish your fly in one small place, you'll need to find a good position and hold it.

There are many places, shallow to deep, where trout may gather: Depressions in the shallows, shoreline cover, channels through water plants, lake-bed springs, and the dark rims of drop-offs are a few such places. Anchoring is usually the answer (see "Anchoring" earlier in this chapter, page 11).

Here, Brian fishes the edge of a small underwater plateau. A modest cast away from it he dropped his anchors, a wise and effective strategy.

SEARCHING WATER

In a broad sense, all fishing to unseen trout is searching. Working a chironomid pupa near the bottom on a long leader and floating line is searching, even though the boat is anchored and casts are all in one direction. It's a slow kind of searching and depends upon moving trout chancing by, which likely they will in an area where chironomids are hatching.

But the searching I refer to here is a fairly orderly combing of likely water. It just makes sense to do this when the trout are scattered, especially if they are moving little. If, however, in your searching you find a cluster of trout, stay with it until the action dies.

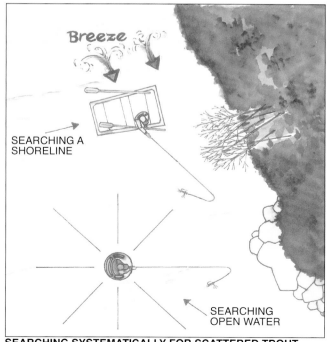

Breeze

SEARCHING A SHORELINE

SEARCHING OPEN WATER

SEARCHING SYSTEMATICALLY FOR SCATTERED TROUT

When trout are in the shallows lying near cover or seeking the sort of insects that gather there—ants and *Siphlonurus* mayflies for example—you can simply let the breeze push your boat or float tube along just out from shore (if those breezes sweep along the shore and not across it). A now-and-then tug on the oars is all you'll need to hold your course in a boat. In a float tube, of course, you can drift or kick or both. Your casts should divide the shoreline into fairly even sections; a cast every two to four feet is usually good.

When searching open water, you can also make your progress on a breeze. Because trout in open water may lie in any direction, make your casts in a circle around your craft, as the hands of a clock travel around its face.

But whether covering shoreline or open water, a wind too strong or from a bad angle means you'll probably need to drop an anchor (or two). Then work some water, raise the anchor, move, and drop the anchor again, in thorough, methodical progress.

INSECT HATCHES

Insects hatch by their own mysterious plan, which often baffles fly fishers. The main things you need to know are (1) hatches are often confined to only part of a lake, a part which may be as large as all the depths below a few feet or as small as a single tiny bay, (2) hatches may vary in volume and length and starting time from day to day, even if all other conditions—temperature, wind, sunshine—remain constant, and (3) specific hatches may come late or early from year to year. For more on the peculiarities of insect hatches, see "The Character of Hatches" in Chapter 7, "Insects and Other Trout Foods," page 42.

STEALTH

The beginning fly fisher generally spends more time frightening fish than catching them. Stealth is what they lack, and what they need—fish that scatter in fear won't soon be caught.

- First, make the last 50 feet or so of reaching your position *especially* quiet—an electric out board in low, oars working smoothly, or fins pumping lightly.
- Second, try to keep your watercraft still as you cast and fish.
- Third, make your casts alight gently if fishing to rising trout. (See Chapter 4, "Fishing the Surface Layer," page 23, for more on fishing to risers.)
- Fourth, walk gently in a boat and avoid any crashing or clanking in any craft. Remember always that trout feel sound rather than hear it. Sounds above the water are of small consequence, unless extreme, but the errant bang of a reel against a boat's floor or the splash of a fin smacking the water will alarm trout further than a long cast away.

THE EXTRA-SECOND LAW

It is my own, the Extra-Second Law, and it evolved in response to errors, frustration, and failure. It says: Slightly slower is faster when action must be quick and precise. For example, a trout makes two quick rises, you know where to cast to meet the third, there is little time to spare; but that's the point: There *is* a little time. Now consider how many things can go wrong: A tailing loop can foul the line, the fly may catch on the boat, both fly and line may crash to the water and frighten the fish, and the fly may miss its critical target. So take that extra second—even half-second—to watch out for trouble and care for your casting. If you do, your fly will likely arrive as it should, where it should, in a relaxed rhythm, rather than the whole delicate sequence collapsing on some snag.

CONFIDENCE

As vague as this thing we call confidence is, its effect on fishing is concrete—a fly fished without confidence is generally far less effective than one fished with it. The angler who believes in his method or fly holds real hope of a strike in every cast, notices every nuance, tests subtle variations. The angler who doubts his method or fly-fishes without commitment, paying little attention and making little effort.

Concentration is a close companion of confidence. Lack the latter and you'll probably lack the former. Concentration enhances learning and improves the catching of fish.

With a dry fly there is often the sight of feeding fish to encourage the angler (though even here, a lack of confidence may cause missed strikes), but usually lake fishing for trout is fishing down in invisible depths, with nothing to inspire. So in the first hours or days of lake fishing, faith must serve where confidence is absent. Time and experience will convert the former to the latter. Begin your lake fishing with faith—in this book, in your flies and tackle, in yourself.

FISHING THE DEPTHS

3

Wfe are talking here mostly of fishing down five feet or more below a lake's surface. And down is where the fishing is best most of the time. When trout are at the surface or in the shallows they are fairly exposed and are tempting loon and osprey and others, which is why trout prefer the relative safety of lying beneath a thick layer of water.

Fishing the depths of a trout lake is Brian's specialty, and he excels at it. Consequently, most of what follows came from him.

COUNTING DOWN

By counting down, especially when fishing from a stationary (which usually means anchored) craft, the angler gauges and adjusts the depth of his line and fly. Counting down with sinking lines, as described below, is common practice.

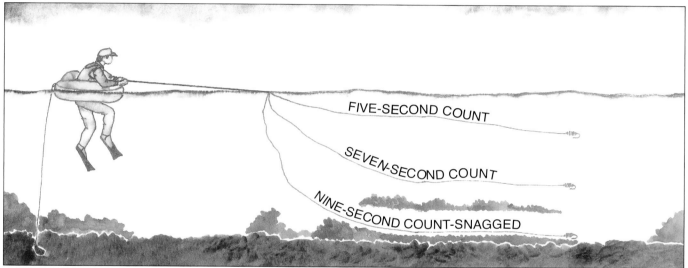

FIVE-SECOND COUNT

SEVEN-SECOND COUNT

NINE-SECOND COUNT-SNAGGED

COUNTING DOWN WITH A SINKING LINE

Counting down: cast out the line, count ("One-one-thousand, two-one-thousand, three. . . " —that's how *I* do it), and then begin the retrieve. Generally it's best to work progressively deeper; in other words, start by retrieving the fly on, say, the count of five; after the next cast, on seven; after the next on nine, and so on until you've found the bottom or trout. You'll likely feel the resistance of the bottom when you find it; if not, the fly may come up with a bit of telling lake-bed plant or debris. Most of the time, trout feed either at the surface or near the bottom. But occasionally they feed in the mid-depths—so explore those too.

Counting down is usually for sinking lines, but it can be a blessing with weighted flies fished deep on floating lines.

The piece of plant-stem on the hook of this fly suggests the sinking line is carrying the fly too deep. The angler probably should shorten his countdown to start his retrieve sooner. If that doesn't work, he should switch to a slower-sinking line. (A quicker retrieve is another possibility, as discussed later in this chapter under "Choosing a Sinking Line.")

THE FLOATING LINE AND DEEP FLY

When speaking at fly-fishing clubs and sportsmen's shows, Brian and I often find audiences hungry for information about "chironomid fishing," working a chironomid-pupa imitation near the bed of a lake, suspended from an indicator off a floating line. They've heard it's deadly, and they've heard right. Here's how it's done.

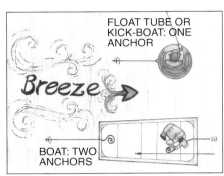

1. The best time to fish an imitation of a chironomid-pupa is during a chironomid hatch (though occasionally such imitations are effective without a hatch). So, look over shoals, especially *mud* shoals, to find chironomids struggling to emerge from their shucks, the glassy shucks they abandon, or both. You might even notice a few adults sailing by. Try to find the heaviest activity.

2. Position yourself in among the hatching chironomids; then slowly and *quietly* drop one anchor if you are in a float tube or other inflatable craft, two anchors if you are in a boat. If you are in a boat and there is any breeze at all, set the boat so the breeze runs down its length, from bow to stern—this will provide the steadiest footing and allow you to fish off the boat's side, which is the easiest way.

3. Using an insect net (or a fine-mesh aquarium net or just your hand), catch up a real pupa. Compare the pupa (quickly—it's about to hatch!) with your flies and find a pattern similar in size and color. (If you can't get a real pupa, scoop up an empty shuck— at least then you'll have the size figured out—then try a brown or black imitation, the most common chironomid-pupa colors.)

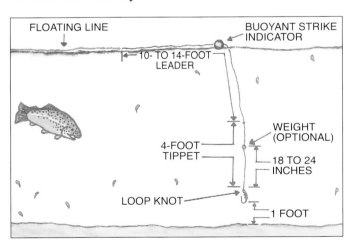

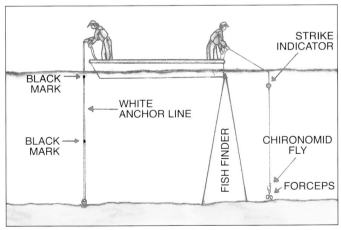

4. Here is the standard rigging for floating line/deep fly chironomid fishing. To a full-floating line, attach a long (normally, 10- to 14-foot) leader, and to that a long (normally, four-foot) tippet. (Specifics are on page 74, under "Leader.") Connect your pupa-imitation to the point of the tippet with a loop knot. If the fly is unweighted—no lead wire or metal bead in its makeup—you may need to add weight 18 to 24 inches up from the fly; Brian prefers lead or lead-substitute putty. Use very little.

5. Now you must determine depth—a critical step. You can just check it on your fish-finder, if you have one, or use a white anchor rope, marked every three feet with a waterproof marking pen, as a gauge; then measure the distance from fly to indicator with one or more spans of your outstretched arms. My full reach is about six feet, and I've used it many times for this work. Another method: clamp your forceps firmly onto the bend of your fly's hook, lower the forceps to the bottom, raise the forceps a foot, set the indicator.

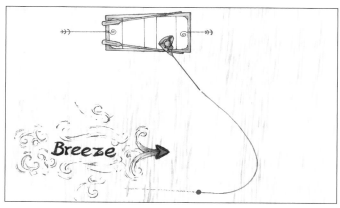

6. Attach a strike-indicator up the leader from the fly a distance just one foot short of the depth—in 14 feet of water, for example, the indicator should be 13 feet up from the fly. (Some designs of strike-indicator, like the little cork ball called the "corkie," must be threaded up the leader before the fly is tied on the tippet.)

7. If there is a breeze, cast well out, at a right angle to the line of the wind, across wind. *Do not* retrieve the fly until line and indicator are *straight downwind*. This will take quite a while. But the whole time, the fly will be working its way down, and then jiggling and drifting just off the bottom, animated by the bobbing indicator.

Whenever the line is out, keep constant watch on the indicator. (Blinking is permissible, but make it quick.) I mean *whenever* the line is out—trout don't always wait for the fly to sink. If the indicator dips, jerks, or just stalls, set the hook immediately and *lightly*.

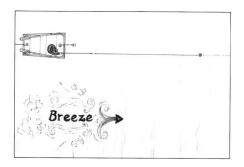

8. When at last the line and indicator are straight downwind, begin the creeping, stalling retrieve detailed on page 58 (#2), under the heading "Chironomids."

9. If the air is still and the lake's surface calm, cast your fly well out, wait for the fly to sink fully (Brian determined, for example, that a size-12 bead-head fly with no weight attached to the leader took 65 seconds to get clear down), and then begin the retrieve detailed on page 58, (#2) under "Chironomids".

I've had excellent fishing with a weighted Skip Nymph below a floating line over weedy shoals during mayfly hatches—essentially, chironomid-style fishing. Brian fishes a weighted imitation damsel nymph this way very early in the hatch. These larger, heavier flies may fish best without an indicator.

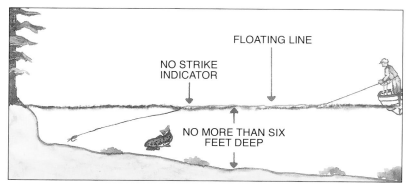

In water down to about six feet deep, a weighted nymph can be worked just off the bottom on a full-floating line. The fly is cast out, counted down (see "Counting Down" earlier in this chapter, page 15) and then retrieved slowly to keep the fly deep. This works with imitations of scuds, leeches, water boatmen, dragonflies, and mayflies.

CHOOSING A SINKING LINE

Before you choose a sinking line to suit the moment, you first must answer these two questions:
1. How deep do I want to fish the fly?
2. How quickly do I want to retrieve the fly?

We'll ignore the floating line because even though a deep fly can be fished on it, it has no sink-rate—fly-line sink-rates are the whole point here.

The answers to these questions are, of course, just guesses. But once you've made your guesses, which provide a starting point, you can select a line-type based on the principles explained in the next caption. (For an explanation of sink-rates for fly lines, see "Fly Line" in Chapter 10, "Boats, Float Tubes, and Tackle," page 73.)

At the same retrieve rate, a type IV (fast-sinking) line will sink much deeper than a type I (slow-sinking) line. But if you retrieve the type IV quickly and retrieve the type I *very slowly*, both will find the same depth.

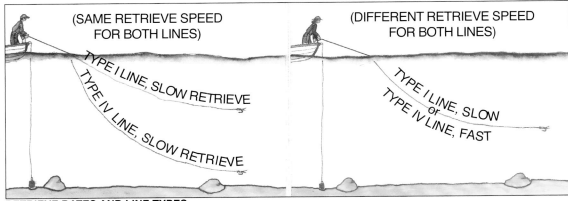

RETRIEVE RATES AND LINE TYPES

TROLLING

Trolling, at times, simply makes good sense. It can also be a relaxing break. My friend Gordon Honey considers trolling the best way to begin on an unfamiliar lake, covering water, free to observe the shuck of a mayfly or sweep of a shoreline.

Some see this as an inferior method. I disagree; I think it has its place. In any case, it is unwise to bad-mouth trolling, for those who do often wind up as red-faced trollers with suspect opinions.

A few important words of advice: (1) use only *full-sinking* lines of at *least* type III (though I admit I've managed with a type II), (2) troll *slowly* so that the line may get down near the bottom (most anglers troll *far* too quickly), and (3) expect to snag the bottom now and then—a good sign that your fly is staying down near that bottom, as it should.

Make a cast; feed out line; in a boat, set the rod so it won't go over with the pull of a trout; in a float tube, tip the rod down. Progress slowly, varying speed slightly—and with that, you are trolling. Your goal is normally to keep the fly near the bottom in water 15 to 25 feet deep. The very best thing about trolling is that it constantly keeps the fly down, working—no waiting for fly and line to sink, no picking them up to cast. The worst thing about trolling is that the angler's part is fairly dull... unless, of course, the fishing is fast.

But trolling needn't always put the fly near the bottom. On a floating line, a nymph can be trolled just under, or a dry fly atop, the surface—just remember that most of the time, trout in lakes feed deep. So don't bother trolling with a floating line unless trout are showing at the surface. (Although anything goes in fishing when orthodox strategies fail.)

When trolling, strip in and check your fly every ten minutes or so—every 15 at most. Even a tiny shard of water plant on the fly renders it useless, an obvious charlatan. Why waste 20 good fishing-minutes without the slightest hope of a strike? To check the fly, just stop, strip it in (making organized coils of line on the boat-floor or float-tube apron), check the fly, clear it if needed, cast it out, and then feed out line as you resume your progress until you are trolling once again.

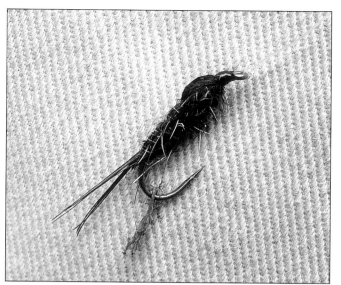

WIND DRIFTING

In Canada "wind drifting" means casting from an anchored craft, and then letting a floating fly line drift with the push and chop of the wind. But what follows is the American definition, and the one I'll discuss from here on.

Wind drifting is, in effect, trolling, but in wind drifting the angler's craft is pushed by wind and not by oars or fins.

Wind drifting is most effective in a boat or high-riding kick-boat—a float tube simply puts everything too low in the water for the wind to have much effect.

A boat or kick-boat will naturally turn sideways to the wind—if the oar on the downwind side (the side away from the wind) is out of the water (where drag can't make it spin the craft around). An outboard motor should be tipped up out of water because it, too, can spin a boat. Sideways is the right way to wind drift, with the line trailing the craft's progress. The angler's hands are free to tease the line and set the hook.

Some working of oars or fins can help control course, and sometimes speed, but it's still a lazy, dreamy way of working a fly. It's also very effective—with the right fly and line.

The drag and weight and wind-resistance of your craft as well as the strength of the breeze all play roles in how fast the fly and line are towed. But a complex formula isn't called for; just use a line that can cut its way to the bottom. (Unless, of course, you want to fish the surface with a floating line.) A strong breeze may require a type IV line, a weak breeze just a type II. But sometimes wind drifting just won't work—the air is too violent or too nearly still, the fly either racing or hanging lifeless.

In a steady breeze, it is common to troll up a lake against the wind, then wind drift back down.

4

FISHING THE SURFACE LAYER

Two main factors determine if trout will feed at the surface: profit and risk. Risk, of life, is naturally their chief concern. But if trout fed only where and when no heron or loon or otter or eagle could reach them they'd starve. Risk is elemental in the life of a trout, and nearly always present. But it is not consistent. Trout somehow know, for example, that a surface ruffled by wind or obscured by darkness offers less risk than one that is neither.

Trout measure profit, the other factor that brings them to or keeps them from the surface, by the effort required to fill their stomachs. Their senses and instincts tell them where they can spend the least energy for the most food. But the angler can only understand the trout's perspective through reason. Questions such as these help the angler understand: How plentiful are the insects at the surface? how large? how hard for the trout to catch? and, of course, would it be more profitable for the trout to feed elsewhere? It's easy to imagine how the answers to such questions influence the trout's choice, even though a question is something a trout could never conceive.

Profit hinges on a balance that varies from lake to lake. In a lean lake with only thinly scattered mayfly nymphs, chironomids, and such along its bed, even a little at the surface looks attractive. But in a rich lake with abundant life below, it takes lots of surface-fare to convince trout to abandon the generous depths to feed where eagles and ospreys and others may feed on them—the latter, of course, is risk again, which is far too important to a trout to ever be ignored.

But this business of balance goes further yet, for even the depths of a rich lake are not always generous, as the depths of a lean lake are not always stingy. If, for example, the larvae of some chironomid species come suddenly squirming en masse from their mud-holes, lake-depths normally bleak may quickly fill trout's stomachs. But lake-depths normally rich in feed can seem nearly barren—leeches and dragonfly nymphs in hiding, scuds concealed deep within tangles of green stems and shoots—for hours or days or even weeks.

As a result, profit and risk are constantly in flux, so finding surface-feeding trout is timing, and luck.

And there are still other factors. Trout seldom feed at a surface that is too warm or poor in oxygen or if algae bloom makes finding insects there too hard. And some factors still we can't define.

But on the whole, it boils down to this: Trout will normally feed at the surface if that is where their prospects are best, provided they feel relatively safe.

In some lakes, surface-feeding is seldom or never sufficient to make for good fishing. In others, trout feed often and hard on top. Most trout lakes offer at least some fishing at the surface that is worthwhile.

When the balance is right and trout do come up, the game becomes one of skill and finesse, played and savored almost entirely through the angler's eyes.

SKIP MORRIS

FINDING SURFACE-FEEDING TROUT

The best thing, perhaps, about surface-feeding trout is that they are easily found—no testing shoals or shallows or the rims of drop-offs with various flies and lines and retrieves in hopes of chancing into fish. The angler need only look for the disturbances feeding trout make in a surface of otherwise even texture.

When you first arrive at a lake, spend at least a full minute scanning its surface. Look for the splashes or, more likely, the widening circular wavelets made by surface-feeding trout.

If you are fishing down, your consciousness extended along line and leader to the deep fly, come back into yourself now and then to check the surface. You may find trout feeding heavily on top, and if so, then that's where the fishing is likely best.

In either case—upon arrival or when your concentration is on the depths—finding surface-feeding trout will result only from watching judiciously for them.

Good places to look for rising trout include stream mouths, bays, over shoals, and around shoreline obstructions. But trout will rise nearly anywhere on most lakes, even clear out in the center with sixty feet or more of depth beneath them—far too deep for most hatching insects. Whether by wind or wing, insects sometimes end up on water far deeper than that from which they hatched, and where they show, often the trout show too.

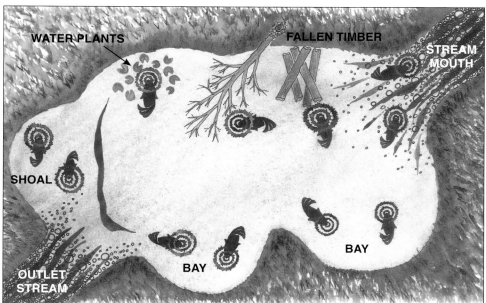

PLACES TO LOOK FOR RISING TROUT

If trout are feeding on top, forget fishing for a minute or two and really examine the surface. Look for nymphs or pupae, discarded shucks, winged adults, things tiny, things big—anything to help you figure out what the trout are taking. Only if you wet the tip of your nose are you looking too closely.

And when you've seen enough to make a guess, choose a fly to match the trout's victims, and then make that fly mimic the victims' actions.

In the faint light of sunset or dawn trout feel free to rise, but that same dimness that protects them then from predator's eyes protects the floating insects from theirs. Therefore, at these edges of daytime, trout are most likely to rise if wind is absent and the surface of the lake is calm. But if there is wind, both you and trout can sometimes escape it in bays or along the lake's sheltered side.

A breeze-ruffled lake-surface obscures trout. During sunlit hours, they appreciate the protection from predators that this provides. But although a light breeze makes the surface more attractive to trout when it's bright out (the opposite of what attracts them in darker hours), they usually find feeding in a heavy wind and at a riotous surface just too much work. Another incentive for trout to feed at a daytime surface—especially a flat one—is shade from clouds.

Be alert for false clues about surface trout. Newts, minnows, splinters of wind, gas bubbles seeping from lake-bed muck, and other such things can mimic the rising of trout and waste the fly fisher's valued fishing time.

Another false clue is leaping trout, not rising or churning or slashing trout—leaping. Trout will rarely leap after insects. Most often, Brian thinks, they leap...well, just to *leap*. But sometimes, he says, it's to shake parasites off their skin.

A FALSE RISE

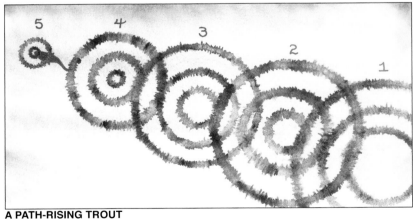

A PATH-RISING TROUT

PATH-RISING AND SEARCHING

Trout feed at a lake's surface in two general ways: path-rising and searching. These terms, at least, are the ones I use. This trout is "path-rising"—gliding just under the surface, tipping up in a fairly steady rhythm, creating a loose pattern in its string of rises. Path-rising occurs most often at sunrise and sunset, when the surface is flat, dim, and frequently littered with insects. But trout may path-rise at a lake-surface, flat or broken, sunlit or dark, at any time.

This trout is "searching"—wandering just below the surface, slowing and speeding and turning on whims, it comes up only when it finds an insect on top. The searching trout offers little, if any, pattern, rhythm, or predictability. But it does stay near the surface, up and feeding.

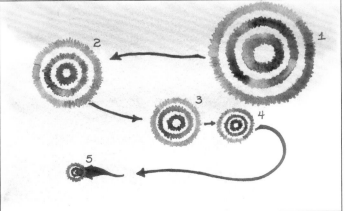

A SEARCHING TROUT

FISHING FOR PATH-RISING TROUT

You have two choices in fishing for path-rising trout: (1) chase them or (2) wait for them to come near. You can wait for path-risers in any kind of craft—sometimes, even wading or standing on the bank—but to chase them you'll need a small light rowboat or a pontoon boat with oars. A pontoon boat for rise-chasing must hold you entirely out of the water, because one that doesn't is just too plodding, and creates too much commotion to let you slip quickly and quietly from position to position. Brian likes to chase path-risers in a boat with a quiet electric outboard motor.

Normally rise-chasing is reserved for path-rising trout, but it can work well for searching trout if they are feeding heavily and frequently showing.

NEXT PREDICTED RISE

WAITING FOR A PATH-RISING TROUT

WAITING FOR PATH-RISING TROUT

To wait for path-risers, quietly take a position near or among them and then watch, and wait. In little or no wind, anchoring may not be required, but anchoring does ensure that you will not drift too far from or too close to the action.

As a trout works near, line up its rises and gauge the span of time and water between them. Now you can estimate where the next rise will come; quietly throw your fly to that spot before the trout reaches it. Make the fly do whatever it should—twitch, swim, lie still—whatever mimics the insects or you think will interest the trout.

When the action slows, just go back to watching and waiting. If the wait grows too long and you sense there is more going on somewhere else, go there.

CHASING PATH-RISING TROUT

To chase path-rising trout, you normally begin by picking out one in particular, one that is staying up and feeding in steady rhythm and is, preferably, not far away.

Next, position yourself to the side and slightly ahead of the trout's rise-path, a 40- to 50-foot cast from where you'll put the fly. Now you are far enough away to not seem a threat, but close enough for an accurate cast and good control of the fly. Being slightly ahead of the trout, you may even manage a second cast if the first fails.

All this is, of course, an ideal. What with turns in rise-paths, drifting boats, breezes, and miscalculations, strategy often crumbles into hasty improvisation.

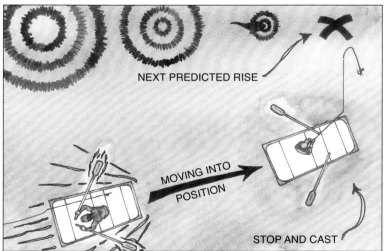

NEXT PREDICTED RISE

MOVING INTO POSITION

STOP AND CAST

CHASING A PATH-RISING TROUT

The most efficient way to chase path-risers is as a team of two. One angler handles the oars (or electric outboard); the other directs and casts. Roles are switched when a trout is hooked or a certain period of time has passed. I seldom find the patience to play the rower, however, so most of my chasing I do alone.

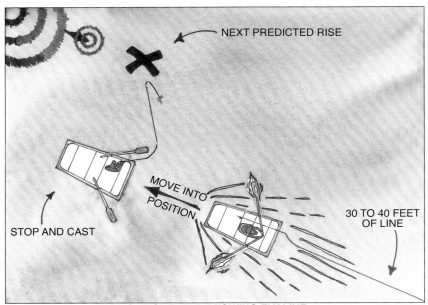

NEXT PREDICTED RISE

MOVE INTO POSITION

STOP AND CAST

30 TO 40 FEET OF LINE

CHASING A PATH-RISING TROUT WHILE TOWING FLY LINE

While chasing path-risers, tow the fly on 30 to 40 feet of line behind you—whatever length of line you can quickly and easily pick up and cast. This eliminates all that time required to strip off line and work it out, and therefore gets the fly quickly and efficiently to the trout. You can leave even more line ready, stripped from the reel, for longer casts; I just sit on the extra line. And make sure the rod is set so a strike to the towed fly won't take the rod over the side. Some set the rod next to them on a boat's flat seat with the reel hanging; this way the reel stops against the seat if a trout tries to steal the whole rig.

CONSIDERATIONS IN CHASING PATH-RISERS

LEADING A PATH-RISING TROUT

The following principles apply equally whether you are chasing path-risers or waiting for them: The more you lead a path-rising trout with your cast, the more chance you take of having misjudged its rise-path; but by putting your fly out well in advance, you give yourself time to make adjustments. A nymph can be hurried or slowed in its travel to wind up right in front of a path-riser; a dry fly can be skidded quickly into place. The trick lies in getting this business completed in time, so, for example, a trout won't see a mayfly spinner that's supposedly almost drained of life scooting along as though strapped to a jet-pack.

But because trout may string their rises neatly and evenly or swim in fits and starts—turning sharply, making the patterns of their rises so ragged that the angler can barely identify them—the angler must always be willing to experiment with how he leads a cruising trout with his fly. But this is quite old news to you by now—I've repeated and repeated through several chapters, perhaps to your annoyance, that flexibility must be the lake fisher's watchword, and to your certain annoyance will repeat it again.

PATH-RISING VARIATIONS

Two factors in how trout path-rise vary greatly: (1) the speed at which they swim and (2) the space between their rises. Moving from rise to rise can be so lazy that to the observing angler the trout seem limp, their bodies gently carried by some light, invisible current; other times it's all business—trout soaring on steady, solid thrusts of the tail at a pace the rowing angler can barely best. But most often these trout swim in easy but earnest rhythms.

The space between the rises of path-rising trout is likely influenced by the speed at which the trout swims. But it's also likely influenced by the space between insects. Consider this: Large insects well scattered on the surface can logically bring only one response from trout—well-spaced rises and a brisk swimming tempo. Moving slowly won't be fruitful—why dawdle for a little when you could bustle for a lot? And rising every foot when the insects are spaced a yard apart means the effort of rising is often wasted. But a tight screen of hatching chironomids across a lake's surface means a trout can fill his stomach best by picking slowly and carefully through the feast.

But however quickly cruising trout swim and however widely they space their gulps, to the angler what matters most is that he notes these variables and adjusts his technique to suit them.

FISHING FOR SEARCHING TROUT

Searching trout can fool you, showing only here and there, seeming to be few when sometimes they are many. I've found trout milling just below sight that were so abundant and intent that a cast in any direction moved one to the dry fly, even though they rarely stirred the surface; at these times floating insects were usually large and few. The explanation for this is probably that these trout were only coming clear up for a find, but otherwise, patiently waiting. Other times near-surface trout were seldom surfacing because they'd chosen to catch the nymphs or larvae just short of the air; but those same trout were perfectly willing to rise to a fully emerged insect adult (or to my dry fly that suggested one) that had slipped past their guard. Sporadic rising is always worth investigating.

But what I've just described are exceptions. As a rule if few trout are showing, it is probably because few trout are there.

But even when you've found trout searching in good numbers, getting your fly within their reach may remain a challenge. You had best be flexible, quick to change tactics, because what works on searching trout one day—even one hour!—may not work the next.

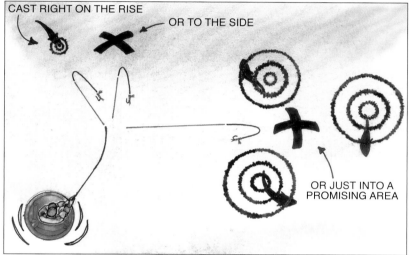

CAST RIGHT ON THE RISE — OR TO THE SIDE — OR JUST INTO A PROMISING AREA

FISHING FOR SEARCHING TROUT

How should you cover the rise of a searching trout? A good question which poses a problem with several good solutions. Finding the best solution for the moment usually calls for experimentation. Sometimes that best solution is to drop your fly right in the rise, right away; sometimes it's to cast to one side of the rise and hope that the trout finds your fly through luck. If plenty of trout are up searching, the best solution may be to simply throw your fly at random out into the broad area in which they are showing.

This casting on luck or a hunch is called "fishing blind," fishing the water instead of stalking a particular fish. Fact is, most fishing in trout lakes is fishing blind—how else can you fish when your fly and the trout are down out of sight?

Again, experiment. There are so many variables—the speed at which the trout swims, how deeply he swings after rising, how thoroughly he inspects the surface. Trying to add all this up is far less efficient than simply trying different strategies.

Positioned near one another, two anglers can work a searcher by casting each to one side of his rise. One fly or the other is likely to lie close enough to the fish to attract it. If both anglers share one boat, this strategy makes even more sense.

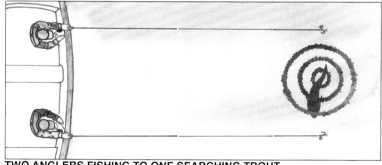

TWO ANGLERS FISHING TO ONE SEARCHING TROUT

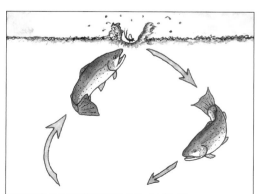

A SPOT-RISING TROUT

"Spot-rising" is my term for an infuriating variation of searching. It means that the trout doesn't mill just under the surface watching for food as a searching trout does; instead, in lunatic fashion, it comes from nowhere, rises, and then returns to nowhere. It's a silly, inefficient thing to do, but trout sometimes do it regardless, especially trout that are smallish or that learned etiquette in a hatchery tank. You can try any of the tactics previously described for searching trout or you can ignore these fools and fish to other trout with more sense.

SHALLOW-WATER FEEDING

In water three feet deep or less, *everything* is near the surface—trout, insects, and the lake's bed. So I felt that shallow-water feeding fell loosely into the topic of this chapter.

Approach shallow trout with great care, especially trout in clear water or bright sunlight, and double that care for trout in both. A long leader; quiet, low, longish casts; a dropping of fly to water with hardly a stir to mark its arrival; the angler almost icy still except for the minimal flick of the cast—successful fishing to shallow trout demands these elements.

Shallow trout, like any trout, may be open-minded or may instead be set on something in particular. If they are the latter, then giving them the fly without arousing their suspicions is only half your task—the other half is figuring out just which fly to give them. In the shallows, as anywhere else in a lake, the nymph is the standard fly. But on occasion shallow trout are seeking something at the surface. As always, observe and experiment and you'll likely figure out enough of what is going on to choose a good fly and make it produce.

Though I've found such occasions rare, it's possible to walk the banks or wade, if the lake's edge or bottom is firm, and actually see the trout you are fishing to. Spotting a trout (the trout itself, not its rise) and fishing specifically to that fish is called "sight fishing." It's high sport, utterly engrossing. Sight fishing requires stealth; polarized sun glasses; fairly clear water; and fairly bright, direct sunlight.

It is also possible (though also rare) to effectively fish a lake's edges *blindly*, wading or walking and quietly casting along the shallow shoreline to unseen trout.

If trout are near shore in clear, shallow water you may, by approaching with care, see them as plainly as you see the one in the center of this photograph. Your challenge then is to show them the fly without showing them you.

If the lake's edges are too marshy or too shallow or generally too awkward for fishing from foot (which usually they are), quietly approach shallow trout in a watercraft. You'll probably have to fish blindly, even where the water is clear, because you'll have to take a position that is too far away from trout to see them—closer would likely alarm them. But covering shallows in this way is usually more effective than wading or walking a lake's edges.

CONSIDERATIONS, COMPLICATIONS, AND OPTIONS IN FISHING THE SURFACE LAYER

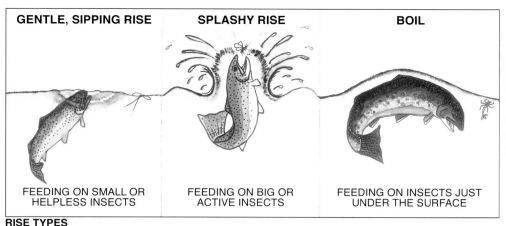

GENTLE, SIPPING RISE	SPLASHY RISE	BOIL
FEEDING ON SMALL OR HELPLESS INSECTS	FEEDING ON BIG OR ACTIVE INSECTS	FEEDING ON INSECTS JUST UNDER THE SURFACE

RISE TYPES

UNDERSTANDING RISE-TYPES

The way a trout rises indicates what he is rising to—it is always to the angler's advantage to recognize the trout's quarry.

MAKING A FLY PERFORM PROPERLY

Despite their heavy hooks and sometimes even additional weight at their core, artificial nymphs sometimes refuse to sink. Casting a floating line to trout that are feeding on mayfly nymphs, chironomid pupae, or whatever lies just beneath the surface is a frustrating exercise when your imitation behaves as a dry fly. (Dry flies, of course, can create this same frustration by behaving like a proper nymph and going right down; the cure for this is described in the paragraph following the next.)

To get that nymph to sink, wipe the leader clean if you suspect any fly floatant on it. Then pinch your nymph firmly under water a few times, and you'll see the culprits, tiny air-bubbles, rise from it.

A dry fly, especially when twitched or tugged, will generally do what the leader and line do—in other words, it sinks if they sink, floats if they float. If they sink, try the following solutions: Replace a floating line that starts to sink (it's old, it's dying—end its misery). Wipe a film of fly floatant on the leader to make it float (and reapply it periodically). Work a tiny bit of floatant into each dry fly before it touches water. And if false casting and dabbing a fly with a cloth and reapplying floatant don't put a soggy dry fly back on top, replace this sodden fly with one fresh and dry.

MISSED TAKES TO DRY FLIES

Everyone misses the takes of trout now and then, either by error or bad luck. Even the keenest anglers expect to miss, or at least lose after hooking, around one out of three or four fish. We are discussing here curing problems that result in only one of every three or four surface or near-surface takes ending in a trout in the net.

Trout often swirl at a big floating insect to sink it; then swing back and take it. Which means that when fishing a big emerger or dry fly, you may have to resist striking at the trout's first attack. The reward will likely be a solid take on the trout's second pass, even if the fly didn't sink as the trout intended.

Remember, too, that it sometimes pays to wait a split second before setting the hook on a dry fly. (See "Striking", in Chapter 2, "General Techniques for Fishing Trout Lakes", page 9.)

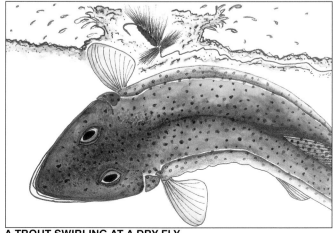

A TROUT SWIRLING AT A DRY FLY

TERRITORIAL RISING

"Territorial rising" is the term I use for trout that are rising within a tight range near cover. That cover can be almost anything—fallen timber, water plants, boulders, a bay, or formations of rock—around which the trout have taken up residence. It often seems trout become territorial simply for security, but sometimes they seem to do it because feed is there, an insect hatch or some land insect falling from shoreline trees.

This riser made a home near the point of this fallen tree; most territorial risers take up residence closer to shore, around water plants, in the shade of outstretched tree limbs, or near any of the cover along the shore of a lake.

Fishing to territorial risers becomes a bit like fishing for shallow largemouth bass: Work the fly around some cover, move a few feet and fish the next likely spot, keep fishing, keep moving.

The difference in working cover for these two very different fishes lies in thoroughness—for bass each likely spot deserves one cast, maybe two, but for trout it's usually best to stay a while, casting and re-casting to a single patch of water. Part of this, of course, lies in the size of the flies—generally, big and obvious for bass, small and easily overlooked for trout. But it's more than that—trout just seem to turn distracted and erratic near cover; rises come without rhythm or plan. Territorial rising usually calls for patience and perseverance. It becomes a matter of working the fly through an area enough times that fly and trout finally connect. Sometimes a lively dry fly is deadly in this situation.

Despite that the former stays near home and the latter is a gypsy, territorial and spot risers are clearly of a kind. (See the description of spot-rising under "Fishing for Searching Trout" on page 25.) With either behavior the angler's best tool is usually experimentation.

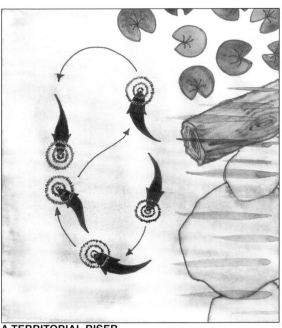

A TERRITORIAL RISER

COVERING A NEAR RISE

NEAR-RISES

When a trout rises close to your float tube or boat (which happens more often than you might suppose), you and your craft should suddenly turn still. The trout will flush at almost any movement so near. I have had trout rise as close as three feet from my boat and have hooked them there. I quickly but quietly drew in most of my line, then made a lazy wrist-only cast, keeping the rod low, moving it no further or faster than required.

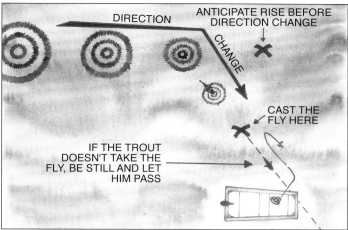

A PATH-RISER CHANGING DIRECTION

(Labels in diagram:) DIRECTION — ANTICIPATE RISE BEFORE DIRECTION CHANGE — CHANGE — CAST THE FLY HERE — IF THE TROUT DOESN'T TAKE THE FLY, BE STILL AND LET HIM PASS

CHANGE OF RISE-PATH

You can be in a fine position to cover a path-rising trout, then find that he has turned away or towards you. If he turns away, you will probably have to move to a new position. If he turns towards you, you may still be able to put your fly in his path without putting him to flight, but remember this: He is now looking in your direction, so cast with particular care and precede his progress a bit extra with the fly. If he passes up your fly, you may have to wait until he is completely past you before you can cast again. A rising trout may pass right under your boat (if the boat is still), and then resume rising on the other side.

THE DRY-FLY OPTION

The fly fisher imitates three general forms of hatching insects with his flies: the underwater form (imitated by an artificial larva, pupa, or nymph); the winged adult form (imitated by a dry fly); and the partly hatched form, somewhere between the first two (imitated by a variety of fly-types, broadly grouped under the title "emergers"). On lakes, imitations of the underwater forms are the most consistently productive. But if you stay strictly with the sunken fly for rising trout, you will miss out on some fine fishing—trout often concentrate on partly or fully hatched insects. Besides, who would want to miss dry-fly fishing on a lake? My advice: Start by collecting imitations of the underwater forms of all the primary insects that hatch on lakes; then build from there by adding emergers and dry flies.

Mayfly spinners, such terrestrials as flying ants, anything that lands on a lake from above, rather than hatching out of it, obviously calls for the dry fly.

NO RISES

Good fishing at the surface usually requires good numbers of trout feeding there. There are exceptions, of course, as when only a few trout path-rise but do so in such earnest that you can pick one, work on it, then go on to the next. When each of these risers has been caught or flushed, it's time to look for deeper trout. Another exception is when shallow trout at the edges, waiting like largemouth bass, prefer the dry fly. You put it near cover, make it shiver and skid, and the trout come from nowhere, trout that had lain quiet before, giving no sign of their presence.

Still, on the whole, don't expect much action fishing the surface when few trout are showing there.

And don't be surprised if insects are hatching but trout are not rising—it's common. It probably means that the trout are down, taking the rising nymphs or pupae. Stay in the area of the hatching and try fishing down.

THE BOTTOM LINE

You need to know that there are lakes—some very productive lakes—in which trout almost never rise. There is just too much below consistently holding their attention. The fishing can be wonderful; it's just not rise-fishing.

5

READING A LAKE

I t is the nature of trout to seek a lake's surface or its bed. So if, for example, trout are feeding in water 12 feet deep, you would normally expect to find them either near the surface or about 10 or 11 feet below it. But trout (and therefore wise anglers) may disregard all this. Sometimes trout that are feeding on rising pupae or nymphs will select a depth somewhere between the surface and bed and meet the insects there. Nevertheless, the floor and ceiling of a lake are far more common places to find a trout than at any other level.

Generally trout go where the food is, unless oxygen content, fear of predators, water temperature, or some other deterrent keeps them away. But they will even brave modest degrees of discomfort and risk if the food is plentiful and attractive enough.

Where the food is and how temperature, oxygen, and such sway the trout will vary from lake to lake. In lake A, for example, the trout feed nearly always on the shoals and along the drop-offs, but in lake B, just a mile down the road, the trout spend all day, every day, among the lily pads; additionally, July finds lake A only productive at sunset but lake B best at midday—believe me, this sort of thing is common. And imagine how much all this can vary in lakes of different elevations or in different parts of the world. And sometimes you'll find lots of trout—consistently—in a place that ought to hold few or none. This means that even the angler with a good grasp on how to identify promising trout-water on lakes—on how to "read" lakes—can run right past feeding trout to fish some likely but currently unprofitable place. Therefore, be flexible and free-thinking about where you will and where you won't find trout in a lake.

FINDING TROUT BY SIGHT

Blindly searching likely water is generally an efficient way to prospect for trout in a lake. Most of this chapter concerns how to identify such water.

But there are other ways to find lake trout, specifically (1) by using a fish finder and (2) by using your eyes.

Rising trout are often easy to spot, especially when sipping or slashing through a lake's calm surface. But when that surface is ruffled by wind, the ripples of a rise are often easily lost in the texture. Actually, sighting rises nearly always requires watchful eyes.

In shallow clear water, even at a lake's very edge, you can sometimes see trout if you carefully watch through polarized sunglasses for them. Even greater than the challenge of fishing to these trout without alarming them is staying calm in their clear and magnificent presence. (Of *course* trout are magnificent, why else would we trout fish?)

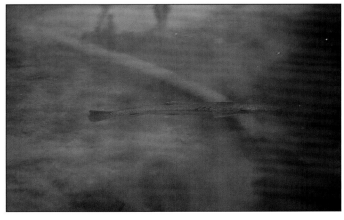

Even in fairly deep water you can sometimes see trout, provided that the water is clear, its surface is fairly smooth, you are wearing polarized sunglasses, and you watch with patience and care.

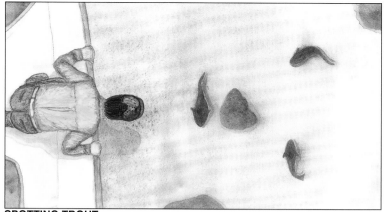

SPOTTING TROUT

FINDING TROUT WITH A FISH FINDER

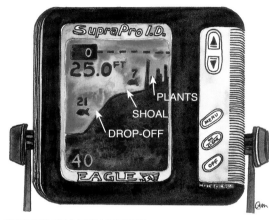

SCREEN OF A FISH FINDER

The fish finder does as its name suggests. Mine identifies fish as tiny fish-shapes and gives the depth of each in feet. But fish finders can be fooled, for example, by limbs on sunken trees, by dense weeds, and by lake stratification. If you own or buy a fish finder, read its instructions to help you accurately interpret its readings.

Actually, what I like most about my fish-finder is that it tells me all about the bed of a lake, all that's down there beyond my sight: shoals, drop-offs, weed beds, mud... I've been frequently surprised to find that the depths of a lake I'd fished for years were nothing as I had imagined them. And as you'll discover, there is great profit for the angler in knowing the depths of a trout lake. (See "Fish Finder" in Chapter 10, "Boats, Float Tubes, and Tackle" on page 74.)

FINDING TROUT BY READING A LAKE

BED-TYPE

On the whole, lake-bed that is covered with plants generally harbors the most insects and attracts the most trout. Rocky bed and bed littered with wood debris are next in line; lake-bed of sand or silt or mud comes last. But remember that each type *can* be productive—mud bed, for example, can produce tremendous chironomid hatches. Most lakes will have a variety of different bed-types. If no particular insect is active, look to the bed with plants first, but if insects *are* active, be it in rock or silt or whatever, that's where you will probably find the trout.

And it's not just in fishing deep that bed-type matters, because most of the insects that hatch do so almost directly above their habitat—the dry-fly fisher, for example, looking for *Callibaetis* mayfly duns should look above the plant-covered lake-bed where the *Callibaetis* nymph resides.

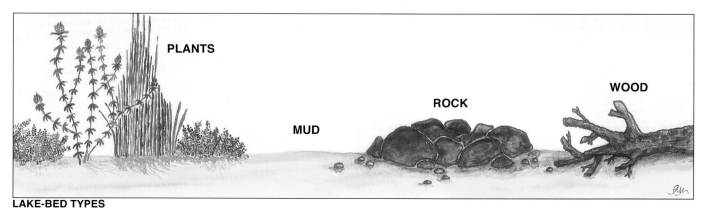

LAKE-BED TYPES

A fish finder can tell you of water plants and suggest a lake-bed of rock or wood debris. Since it indicates the density of the bottom, it can even help an experienced operator guess at sand or mud.

But there are still some good, primitive methods for identifying bed-type. A bit of plant or wood retrieved on a deeply fished fly tells. And pay attention to the evidence your anchor retrieves—this one clearly found a bed of vegetation.

EDGE COVER

Because there is often both food and cover around the edges of lakes, trout will sometimes be there. Of course not all lakes have this cover and not all lakes that have it have it all around their shorelines. But when the trout are in it, they are concentrated in a fairly slim, shallow band, and fishing can be excellent. Spring and fall are the likeliest times for water-temperatures and oxygen-content to attract the trout to the shoreline, but I've seen it every month from early spring to late fall. Shoreline trout nearly always call for the floating line, or perhaps the very slow-sinking type I line.

Tree branches that hang over a lake's edge provide cover for trout, and habitat for both land- and water-insects upon which trout may feed.

Trees newly fallen out into a lake may still be green with needles or leaves; trees long ago fallen may be veiled in a gray tangle of bare branches. Ultimately, all end up as naked bones decaying on a lake's bed. But at any stage, a tree fallen into a lake is a good place to prospect for trout.

Bulrushes, lily pads, and other shallow water plants provide cover for insects and trout. Sometimes it pays to fish all around and even right in through this tangle. If you've ever fished for shallow large-mouth bass, you may find this type of trout fishing familiar.

WATER-PLANT CHANNELS AND POCKETS

Yes, I just told you about water plants near shore as a place for trout, but that's not what I refer to here. Here I'm talking about big beds of plants that reach well out into a lake and may not even connect with the shoreline.

In some shallow lakes, or the shallow parts of deep lakes, it is common practice for trout fishers to hunt the channels and pockets in dense growths of water plants. For these channels and pockets, a floating or type I full-sinking line is usually best, and the trout—in clear water, tight quarters, and under flat patches of open surface too small for the wind to stir—are nervous. Present your fly to the trout with care.

UNDERWATER BEDS OF PLANTS

In a clear lake, you can see sunken beds of water plants if they're not too deep. Deeper beds, or those in stained-water lakes, you'll find by experimentation, experience, or with a fish finder. Because insects live in these beds, they are always good places to prospect for trout. Work a fly down over them and around their edges.

BAYS

Any indentation, large or small, along a shoreline is a bay. Bays seem to attract trout, at their ends, which are often points (see "Points," which follows), and throughout, and at a variety of depths.

Bays, seeming private and pleasant and being often a place to escape heavy wind, also attract anglers. Some bays even contain a productive shoal across their middle.

POINTS

As the name implies, a point is simply a finger of land (like any finger it may range from bony thin to bulging fat) sloping down and pointing out into a lake. Trout often collect at varying depths around points.

Like most points, this one is really a ridge that continues down into the lake.

FEEDER STREAMS

When the heat of long summer days penetrates and warms a lake, it's the cool water of feeder streams trout seek. But even when the lake is comfortable to trout, a stream may attract them into its flow by pouring in a hatch of current-loving insects. And sometimes trout seem to gather at the mouths of streams for no apparent reason. Trout at a feeder stream may lie shallow or deep, well up into the current or out so far that the current is barely perceptible.

Be it a large river or tiny streamlet, its entering-point into a lake can attract trout. Some streams spit out abruptly at a right angle to a straight shoreline. Others gradually lose their force down long, slowly widening arms blending, finally, into lake-stillness.

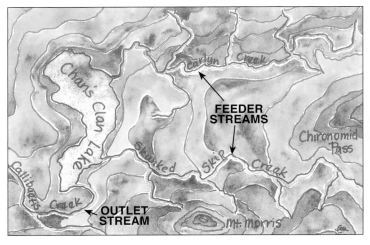

A map can help you locate feeder streams.

SHOALS

A shoal is essentially an underwater plateau. Shallow enough that light may reach and nourish life upon it, yet deep enough that trout may prowl it in relative safety, a shoal's gentle slope tends to grow such water plants as chara, potamageton, and milfoil along with lots of insects, this last being the trout's real interest. Some shoals rise up from deeper water, but most taper gradually down from shore. The day in-day out best fishing depth on shoals is around six to 15 feet. But shoals can be as shallow as one and one-half feet deep to as deep as 18 feet and at times trout will seek both these extremes.

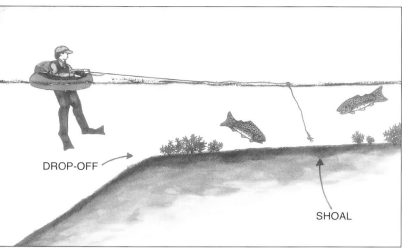

A SHOAL

Shoals that are heavy with underwater plants produce the greatest numbers of insects in the greatest diversity. A weedy shoal can thrive with mayfly, damselfly, and dragonfly nymphs, backswimmers, caddis larvae, scuds, and more.
This abundance and variety tends to attract trout more often than the modest assets and scant selection of other shoal-types.

But welcome to fishing—the world of soft rules and exceptions...

One shining exception to the weedy-shoals-are-best rule is the mud shoal with its frequently copious crop of chironomids. A mud shoal can be an excellent place to fish; it's just a matter of timing. Besides, shoals primarily of mud or stone or anything-but-plants often have patches of plants sprinkled across them, just as weedy shoals may have plenty of mud or wood debris or whatever beneath the green camouflage.

To the wise lake fisher, all shoals hold promise.

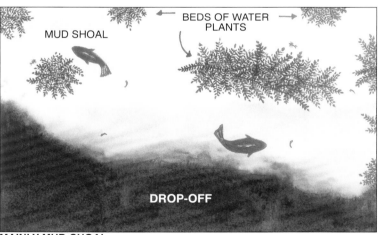

MAINLY MUD-SHOAL

Here is a broad shoal; the dark water at the top of the photo is where the shoal abruptly ends and the drop-off begins. In the clear water of this lake, the shoal and drop-off are obvious; in the tinted water of many lakes, such features are hidden. Not all lakes contain true shoals, and many contain only a few small ones, but wherever there are shoals in a trout lake, there is a good chance trout are on them.

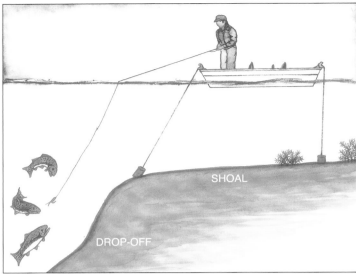

DROP-OFF

DROP-OFFS

Brian says that when the trout of his Kamloops lakes aren't prowling the shoals or up probing the surface, they are often hanging just beyond the edges of the shoals at the beginnings of the drop-offs. The drop-off is where the bottom turns steeply down into deeper water. Drop-offs along shoals are convenient for trout, which can move easily onto the shoal to feed on its bounty, then slip quickly back to the safer, deeper water lying just past its rim. In a clear lake, a drop-off often appears as the darkness at the edge of a pale, green, or dappled shoal.

Trout often hang and feed along the edge of a drop-off, slipping occasionally up on the shoal to investigate. If trout seem vacant from the surface, shallows, or shoals, try fishing along the drop-offs.

SPRINGS

Underwater springs often appear as clean sandy patches on a lake's bed; that is, they appear if water-clarity allows—hidden beneath stained water, springs can be elusive, and they are impossible to see on a fish finder. Some springs, however, reveal themselves by releasing a constant stream of bubbles. In too-warm summer water, especially in shallow lakes and reservoirs, trout will gather around a spring's cool oxygen-rich flow. But springs are nearly always good places to search for trout, regardless of water-temperature or the time of year.

UNDERWATER SPRING

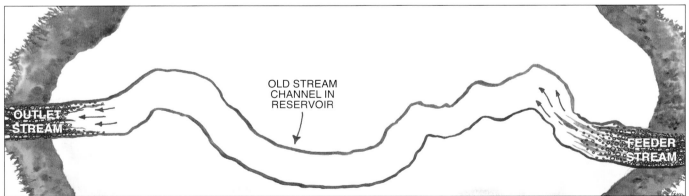

OLD STREAM-CHANNEL IN A RESERVOIR

STREAM-CHANNELS

If it looks as though the only effect a feeder stream has had on a lake's structure is to have bitten into its edge, look further. Often a channel—cut into the exposed bed of the lake during dry seasons—will run well out into the lake. This depression can attract trout. Old stream-channels long drowned may run the length of a reservoir. A stream-channel is a good place to seek trout during the hot months, or at any time in shallow lakes.

AN ILLUSTRATED SUMMARY

Below is an imaginary lake containing all the features discussed in this chapter. (Many lakes will have some, lack others.) The standard productive places to fish are identified below with fish symbols. But never strictly limit your fishing in lakes to the standard places.

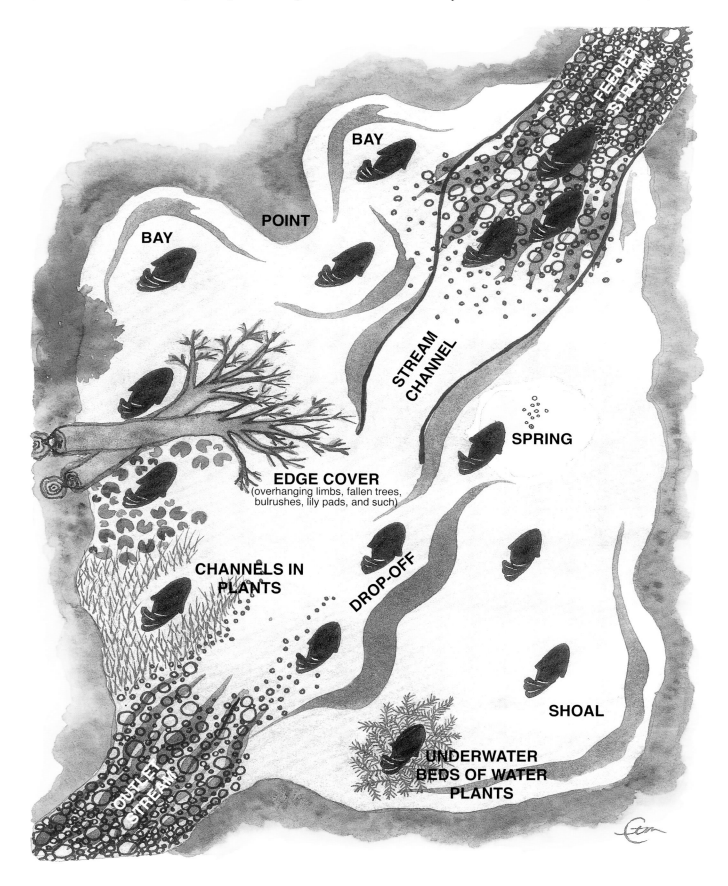

THE LIFE OF A TROUT LAKE

TROUT SURVIVAL

To understand what survival means to trout is to...well, to understand trout. Survival dictates nearly everything trout do. And the greatest threat to that survival, despite so many imposing others—starvation, disease, predation, hot and cold extremes—is insufficient oxygen. The following are key factors in a lake's balance that determine if oxygen content will smother every trout, smother only some, or support them all.

Temperature: Trout avoid warm water because it can hold little oxygen. In mid-summer, it is the surface of a lake that warms most. A shallow lake may warm throughout, killing trout by overheating or smothering them. Extreme cold creates another chain of dangers to trout, as you'll see in the next two topics.

Ice: Lakes may freeze for several weeks or even months in winter, especially lakes at high elevations, at longitudes well north or south, or both. The cap of ice creates a barrier to oxygen. The snow that commonly blankets that ice creates a barrier against light, killing the oxygen-producing plants of warmer months and reducing oxygen even further. Finally, the bacteria creating the decay of those plants demands yet more of the now-finite oxygen supply. If all this thins the oxygen too much before the ice melts in spring, trout die.

Turnover: At "ice-off," which means exactly what it suggests, most of the lake's remaining oxygen is concentrated near the surface and usually in short supply. The coldest water is also at the surface (it's still barely warmer than ice), but spring will warm the surface until, finally, the lake will be one temperature, and therefore one density, throughout. Now there is no lateral banding of different temperatures, no "stratification"—when winds pull at the surface, the lake begins a massive sluggish rotation known as "turnover." Turnover mixes the free unstratified water, in turn, dispersing the oxygen. If too little oxygen gets spread too thin, again, trout die. Shallow lakes do not turn over—they are too flat to rotate. Turnover can come again, months later, with fall's cooling weather.

Bloom: In many rich lakes, warming water may trigger a bloom of algae. Such blooms, if thin, look like fine lawn-trimmings in the water; if heavy, they turn the water nearly opaque, and may be so dense that they pile up as green sludge against the shore. This algae consumes oxygen (at night) and if it leaves too little for the trout, they die. It also blocks light, killing plants which are then decayed by oxygen-consuming bacteria, in turn suffocating trout.

Well, that was all very depressing. Let's move on to more hopeful topics.

Wind: Although it can cause turnover which can kill trout (see "Turnover" above), wind raises the waves that churn oxygen into a lake. Wind right after ice-off can therefore be both threat and salvation to trout.

Feeder Streams: Any time that oxygen in a lake is scarce—beneath winter's ice, at turnover, during algae bloom, when water is too warm—a feeder stream supplies cool oxygen-rich water to desperate trout.

Heavy algae-bloom on a trout lake. Though a possible threat to trout, a bloom indicates a fertile lake.

THE SEASONS, THE TROUT, AND THE ANGLER

If you skipped the section titled "Trout Survival" on the previous page, you may be occasionally confused by what follows. The solution, of course, is to go back and read. (It's one page, large print; won't take long.)

Spring: Usually, lakes that spend winter sheathed in ice, dark beneath thick snow, are set free sometime in spring. When the ice draws back, becomes a shrinking white-edged outline of the lake, anglers eagerly work the ribbon of open water along the shore. They know that the trout, wakened by the warming weather, are hungry after a long winter of lethargy. Best of all (for anglers) oxygen is concentrated near the surface and so, therefore, are the trout—this oxygenated layer seldom reaches more than 12 feet down, often considerably less. Not all lakes fish well at ice-off, but because their trout are hungry and confined, many do.

Fishing will be good until the lake turns over (if it's deep enough to do so); after that is a wretched time for trout (and fishing): everything in turmoil; water fouled with swept-up rotting blackened leaves, clouded with fine decay; and worst of all, oxygen may be barely sufficient.

After ice-off and before turnover, trout will stay near the oxygenated surface, over water from shallow to deep—surface temperature is comfortable throughout the lake. After turnover and its poor fishing, trout settle into their vigorous springtime rhythm. They may feed at the surface, in the shallows, or as deep as they wish. The angler looks for concentrations of trout, because with the full range of the lake now open to them they can be too scattered to provide good fishing. But they are certainly feeding, to shake off winter's fasting, and they've had icy months to forget about flies and anglers so they're likely to be reckless, the easiest they'll be all season.

Insects come alive in the warming water. Most insects hatch in spring and early summer, so as spring progresses, their hatching increases. (See Chapter 7, "Insects and Other Trout Foods.")

Lakes that don't freeze contain good oxygen levels all winter long, so spring probably won't find trout forced up near the surface. Such lakes can still turn over in spring but, perhaps because of all that oxygen, fishing can be good right through a turnover that's modest. But spring on any lake is always a time of hungry trout freely prowling all depths and responding to intensifying insect hatches. And fishing can be good any time of day, or all day long...or, of course, not at all...that's fishing, you know.

Summer: At some point during summer, on most lakes, fishing hits a slump. It does so partly because the trout have grown wise to anglers and flies. But it does so mostly for these two reasons: (1) springtime insects—mayflies, caddisflies, damselflies and others—are largely finished hatching and (2) the water is now so warm as to make the trout sullen. There is still hope of good fishing when the lake cools and can then hold more oxygen—specifically, morning and evening. Egg-laying chironomid adults and hatching pupae can be heavy then. Where it's legal, night-fishing can be terrific. But midday generally is a bust (that's generally—this is fishing we are talking about, right?). And you can mostly (but only "mostly") forget the shallows—they're too warm.

One occasional exception is when the angler finds and fishes just above the "thermocline," that cool layer that lies directly beneath the good oxygenation in a stratified summer lake. The angler searching for a thermocline can find it with a thermometer—where temperature suddenly plunges. Expect to find it around 15 to 20 feet deep, but it can be much deeper. The trout may feed atop a thermocline even on hot midsummer days. Or they may just lie there disregarding insects (and therefore, flies) in anticipation of sunset or nighttime feeding.

Another exception can be a spate of cool weather which can set the trout feeding at any time of day.

Fall: Days shorten, nights cool as summer turns to fall. Insects that hatch in fall are few but because trout somehow know that months of icy hunger approach, they are suddenly quite interested in even minor hatches. As the weather cools further, insects move their hatching toward times that are warmest until, finally, midday to early afternoon is prime hatch-time. But with hatches down and trout aggressive, non-hatching insects and creatures—scuds and leeches and such—reach their height of importance. Eventually, deeper lakes turn over, briefly halting good fishing, but soon the trout are again feeding hard. Fall's cool water, like spring's, gives trout permission to range freely—shallows can be productive, as can depths and the surface. Also as in spring, trout lose much of their caution—winter is close at their back and the need for plenty results in haste. This fast, easy, steady fishing (again, no guarantees) can continue right up until the lake freezes.

Winter: In winter, fly fishers have no use for lakes that freeze over. But, of course, some lakes do not.

All the lakes of Brian's Kamloops region freeze and all the good lakes in my area are closed to winter fishing, so Brian and I had to look outside for information on fishing winter trout lakes. We studied books and tapped the experience of Dave Hughes, author of *Strategies for Stillwater*, and Andy Burk, who every winter fishes the trout lakes of Northern California.

As described at the beginning of this chapter, winter means hardship—sometimes death—to trout in lakes that freeze. In lakes that don't, it's still no vacation—nearly all edible things are hidden, and frigid water drains the vitality of trout to near-sleep. But warm winter weather can stir trout in ice-free lakes to real aggression.

Dave has found fishing on trout lakes in winter mostly to be a matter of dragging a deep fly around until some drowsy trout finally responds—a miserably dull and unproductive business overall. But he has also found that the mildest days can move chironomids to midday hatching, resulting in some truly worthwhile fishing.

Many of Andy's California lakes are fed by springs, providing fairly constant water-temperature the year round, with fishing fairly constant, too. On what he calls "false-spring days," winter chironomid fishing spans nearly all the daylight hours. These are chironomids on the small side of the scale, imitated with hooks size-14 down to size-24. Dry and emerger flies with floating lines are often good on his winter lakes; other times it's the deep fly that produces. Either way, the midday hours, the warmest hours, are the dependable winter times to fish.

If Andy's description of winter fishing on unfrozen lakes sounds more promising than Dave's, bear in mind that what Dave describes is the more typical.

WEATHER

Though we touched on this two pages ago, that first discussion pertained to trout survival; here it pertains to day-to-day fishing.

First to consider are the seasons—what kind of weather will please the trout this particular time of year? If the trout are too cold they'll want warm weather, if they are too warm they'll want cool. (See "The Seasons, the Trout, and the Angler" earlier in this chapter.) The important thing is that the water comes at least near that ideal range for trout: about 50° to 65° Fahrenheit. Wise lake anglers carry and use a thermometer.

The barometer is another matter. When it's falling, and weather worsening, fishing is usually poor. When it's stable or rising, and weather stable or improving, regardless of what kind of weather that is, fishing is usually best. Carrying a small barometer is a wise policy.

Though not really "weather," the phases of the moon seemed to fit here. A full moon tends to bring good fishing at night, poor fishing during the day, and the effect is greatest during the hottest months of summer.

FERTILITY

There is much to consider in evaluating a lake's potential for growing trout—acidity, dissolved solvents, nutrients and such. Too much, perhaps, to interest someone other than a fisheries biologist (my co-author, Brian, for example). There are textbooks on the subject if you wish to investigate further, but I'll just say that geology and fate can make lakes in different parts of the world—even in different locations in a single square mile—very different in regards to how the trout in them grow.

STAGNATION AND SPAWNING

Stagnation is often misunderstood. Contrary to what you may have heard, a lake with no feeder or drainage stream, a "stagnant" lake, can be a marvelous producer of trout. Conversely, a stream-fed lake can be putrid.

Then there's spawning—trout can't do it without flowing water. But who cares if a lake is streamless when it grows hefty planted trout?

TIMING

Good or bad fishing is a matter of skill, timing, and luck. Lakes have bad hours, bad days, bad months, and even bad years. They have good ones, too. Your chances of hitting a lake at a good fishing time should be vastly improved by reading this chapter and this book. Just be aware that much of the life of a lake is beyond the puny mind of puny man.

INSECTS AND OTHER TROUT FOODS | 7

Lakes, even the least productive ones, contain a remarkable variety of insects and other creatures that trout eat. There are delicate mayfly and damselfly nymphs among the water-plants, wormlike chironomid larvae burrowed into the silt, stout caddis larvae lumbering openly in the cases they construct, big dragonfly nymphs on the prowl, swimming snaky leeches, dogpaddling scuds, and others. From the thin shallows out across the sloping shoals and down into considerable black depths there is miniature life going about its business of feeding, mating, dying, and being born. It's a complex and colorful world that can grab your imagination if you give it half a chance. But at the least you need a practical understanding of the insects and other things trout seek in a lake if you're going to fish lakes effectively.

Anglers often fish flies that imitate the creatures trout see all the time—dragonfly nymphs and leeches that hunt, scuds that just putter around—and this can make for some excellent fishing. But the best fishing usually comes with a hatch.

A "hatch" is a mass migration of a particular insect-type from water to air. When each insect reaches the water's surface, it struggles free of its now-loosened outer skin, its "shuck," extends and dries its new wings, and flies off.

Trout get onto hatches. All those insects moving to the surface are easy prey. So, naturally, fly fishers try to be there when hatches occur.

There are two basic life cycles of hatching insects. Chironomids and caddisflies live most of their lives under water as a *larva,* change just before hatching-time to a *pupa,* and then swim up and hatch as a winged *adult.* The adult flies off to mate, and (if it's a female) returns within hours or days to the water to deposit its fertilized eggs.

Mayflies, damselflies, and dragonflies, on the other hand, live most of their lives under water as a *nymph,* which heads for the surface at hatching-time, emerges from its shuck there, and flies off. (Mayflies, damselflies, and dragonflies all migrate to the surface differently.) The mayfly emerges as a *dun* and matures to a *spinner,* while the adult of the damselfly and dragonfly is simply called an *adult.* The mature adult female later flies out onto the water with her fertilized eggs.

The fly fisher must understand hatches in order to fish them effectively—knowing when and where to find them, how to fish them, and which fly patterns are effective for them.

Some important insects and other creatures that trout eat don't hatch at all—waterboatmen and backswimmers swim under the water or scurry atop it or fly off and then plop back into it whenever they like; scuds and leeches just live beneath the water their entire lives.

THE CHARACTER OF HATCHES

First, you must know that insect hatches are seldom unmistakable; they rarely involve some display of motion, mass, and purpose that seizes the attention, like a great run of salmon in an Alaskan river. Instead, hatches are usually subtle, often nearly invisible. Watch for them carefully and you'll find them; watch casually and most will pass undetected.

The signs of a hatch are predictable: birds swooping at a lake's surface or pecking about the reeds; nymphs or pupae rising from below; sloughed-off insect-shucks around the shore or on the water; insect-adults sailing by on new wings; and sometimes trout gently probing or slashing at the surface.

But don't be surprised if those signs are confined to certain small or large areas of a lake, because hatching insects, too, are confined to just those parts of a lake that suit them.

Insect hatches can be moody, waxing and waning with little regard for schedules concocted by man. They are often light when they should be heavy, heavy when they should be light. Even more, they are sometimes absent when all conditions are prime. And once in a while they will burst in abundance at utterly wrong times of season or day. So it's hard to make rules or even lay down guidelines for hatches, for to do so is to see your words turn to lies again and again. Which, in turn, is why close attention to hatch-signs (and, of course, observation in general) is critical to good fishing.

Here's an example of just how unpredictable insect hatches can be. A few days ago my friend Gordon Honey, the fly-fishing guide, his clients, and I chased hatches of *Callibaetis* mayflies all over a Canadian lake. We began by fishing a little bay amid raindrops, mayflies, and feeding trout from around 1:30 to just after 2:00 p.m. Then the mayflies slowed and the trout disappeared. On a whim, I ran to a shoal Gordon had showed me, and again found mayflies and trout. I waved and yelled across a half-mile of lake until Gordon and his clients came. For another two hours the action was back. Then things slowed again. Wet, cold, and satisfied, I quit. When Gordon finally knocked on the door it was 6:00. He said he'd found mayflies again on yet another bay, had dropped off his clients just before 5:00, and had then gone back out just to see how late the mayflies would come. "Just ten minutes ago," he said, "they stopped, finally."

A MAYFLY SHUCK

Callibaetis mayflies are supposed to stop hatching by midafternoon. Never at ten-to-six.

Why did the hatch keep fading out here, then fading in there, rather than everywhere all at once? And why was it brief at the first bay, then more than twice as long at the shoal, and then even longer at the last bay? And why did it ultimately continue far later than it should have? *Why?*

You can make yourself half-crazy with whys, keeping notebooks, postulating theories, starting over again and again when your towers of evidence keep toppling. Notebooks and theories are well and good; sound, useful information can come from them. But the keenest and most experienced lake fishers I know make only rough predictions about insect hatches, and make them with only the flimsiest commitment.

A CHIRONOMID SHUCK

Hatches usually bring feeding trout, and the heavier the hatching, the heavier the feeding. But sometimes a hatch comes off in abundance and the trout take no notice. Why? Perhaps it has to do with oxygen or temperature, perhaps some other form of food is even more abundant elsewhere, or perhaps the trout fed all the previous night and are full.

But perhaps it is sometimes better not to ask why, and simply to accept.

That's how it is with hatches—they sort of follow the rules mostly, but sometimes don't follow them at all. The trout-lake fly fisher must be generally flexible and observant, and so he must be specifically with hatches.

CREATURES TROUT EAT THAT HATCH

CHIRONOMIDS

Putting chironomids first was an easy decision—trout in lakes probably eat them more often than anything else that hatches. And Brian's position as a leader in the chironomid cult made it logical to do so.

Though infamously tiny in rivers, chironomids in lakes can be big. That alone gives them importance, but also they hatch in abundance, clear through the year. Spring and fall are usually the best chironomid times. Then, they hatch around comfortable midday. Summer's heat moves the hatching towards cooler dusk and dawn.

The chironomid's life has three stages: larva, pupa, adult. It lives nearly everywhere around this Earth, and it can live nearly anywhere within a lake—wood debris, plants, stones. But most abundant are the mud-dwelling species, thriving where little else can or will.

Chironomid colors vary. Here are the most common in order of frequency: black, brown, red (yes *red*!), tan, green, and cream. This order applies to every stage.

The tiniest match a 24 hook, the largest are matched with an eight (and, I've heard, even size-6!). In Canada the eights and the tens are called "bombers." Sizes 16 to 12 are most common.

The chironomid larva lives shallow to deep—from water only a few feet deep down to 50 feet or more. But expect it most often from six feet to 20. And expect it to live in mud, though it can live nearly anywhere along a lake's bed.

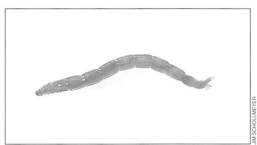

CHIRONOMID LARVA

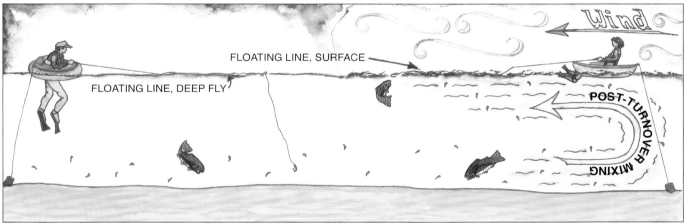

FISHING A CHIRONOMID-LARVA MIGRATION

The following information comes from Brian's years of studying chironomids.

Chironomid larvae, though usually hidden from trout, migrate in spring—squirming, clumsy, exposed—seeking shallower places for warmer months. In the fall this migrating goes in reverse. Some species of chironomid larvae never migrate; thus throughout the season larvae are scattered from shallow to deep.

Fishing this migration calls for a floating line, long leader, and imitation larva (see Chapter 8, "Flies for Trout Lakes," page 60). The technique is the same one used for an imitation-pupa. Fish patiently, knowing the movements of the larvae are minor, their progress slow. (See "The Floating Line and Deep Fly" in Chapter 3, "Fishing the Depths," page16.)

If larval migrations come soon after turnover, spring or fall, the larvae can be swept to the surface. It happens after the water has cleared yet remains even in temperature throughout its depths, so that winds may stroke the great body of the lake into a sluggish spin. Lower your face to the water's surface; look closely and you'll see them, sometimes up so high they seem to bump against the air—stubby worms, squirming, helpless.

The floating-line-deep-fly approach may work then too, if the trout are hunting the bottom. But sometimes the trout seek these displaced larvae on top. If so, cast your fly to the rises; leave it still or twitch it only a little. (See Chapter 4, "Fishing the Surface Layer," page 20.)

The larva turns to pupa, the pupa is buoyed to the surface by gas in its shuck, the shuck is discarded, wings unfurl, dry, and the new adult takes flight.

CHIRONOMID PUPA

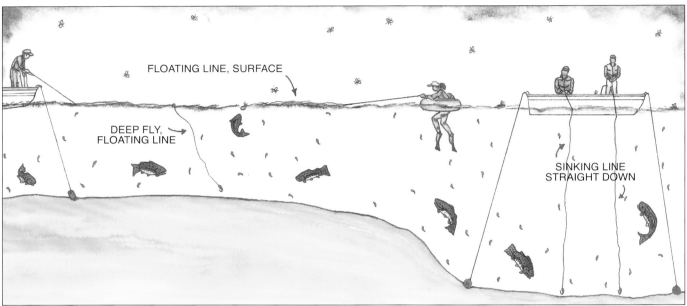

FLOATING LINE, SURFACE

DEEP FLY, FLOATING LINE

SINKING LINE STRAIGHT DOWN

FISHING A CHIRONOMID HATCH

If chironomids are hatching but trout are not rising—which is quite common in daylight—reach down with a long leader and floating line. (See "The Floating Line and Deep Fly" in Chapter 3, "Fishing the Depths," page 16.) If chironomids are hatching and trout *are* rising (in significant numbers), use a dry-fly adult, a half-dry emerger, or a pupa-fly barely submerged. (The last two are the best bets.) Cast one of these on a floating line to rises. Leave it still or move it just barely now and then.

For the deepest chironomid hatches (around 25 to 30 feet deep), anchor the boat, cast straight out with a full-sinking line of type III (no slower sinking than type II), let the fly sink to straight down, then slowly work it back up. This method is unique to chironomid fishing.

The chironomid adult has the mosquito's looks but lacks the mosquito's bite. Trout can catch pupal and emerging chironomids easier than they can catch adults with wings for escape. So the new adult is rarely the target. But "rarely" doesn't mean "never."

The returning female adult is another matter. She returns in the morning or evening to buzz across the surface, dropping her eggs. Then an imitative dry fly, skidded and stalled, is effective.

CHIRONOMID ADULT

MAYFLIES

Mayfly species are numerous in streams, but in lakes there are only a few. Of these few, only one, *Callibaetis*, is well-distributed. But where mayflies exist, they often abound.

Mayflies live most of their lives under water as a nymph; which struggles from its shuck to become a "dun" (the dun is the freshly hatched adult); and later sheds its skin again to become a fully mature "spinner." The female spinner returns to the water with her fertilized eggs to start the next generation.

CALLIBAETIS

Callibaetis is commonly known as the speckled spinner or speckled dun. It prefers clear (clear, at least, when the insect is hatching), still, or slow-moving water, and it is seldom abundant in any other kind. Turbid or stained-dark water holds few. It matures quickly and can hatch in up to three generations per year—one in spring, one in early summer, one in fall—though two per year is more common, and only one of those may be ample enough to interest trout. These generations may lap and blur or be separate and distinct. And each new generation is smaller—in spring an imitation dun may require a hook of size-12; in summer, size-14; and in fall, a size-16.

This is the lake mayfly so well distributed, from North America's west coast across to its east.

The mature *Callibaetis* nymph is mottled, tan-brown to green; it is slender, and has three tails. It prefers to live among plants at the bottom, from the shallows to around 25 feet deep—its most common range of depth is five to ten feet. At hatch time it swims to the surface out in the open.

***CALLIBAETIS* NYMPH**

The dun is gray or tan or olive on its underside (the side trout see), with mottled wings and two tails. Trout often take it as it dries its wings at the surface. The *Callibaetis* duns of spring begin their hatching around noon to 2:00 p.m. Summer duns are earlier—10:00 a.m. is common. Fall duns, like those of spring, begin hatching around midday. All *Callibaetis* duns like dark days—they'll even start and stop their hatching as the sun departs and then returns with each cloud's passing. Sometimes they want more than clouds, settling only for evening-dark days that threaten rain. They don't mind modest winds, and may even prefer them.

***CALLIBAETIS* DUN**

The speckled leading edge of the otherwise glassy-clear wings of the *Callibaetis* spinner inspired its nickname: the speckled spinner. Its underside is commonly gray, sometimes tan or brown.

Usually in evening (though it seems they'll do it almost any time), female spinners fly out over the lake to release their eggs, then collapse on the water and die. But don't be fooled by swarms of spinners in their amorous aerial afternoon bobbing—none of these is likely to touch the water and tempt trout until the females' egg-laying journey about five days later.

Cast a dry-fly spinner to trout's rises or rise-paths on a still lake-surface in evening calm (sometimes very early in the morning), and make that fly quietly mimic the insect's dying shudders.

***CALLIBAETIS* SPINNER**

FISHING A MAYFLY HATCH

FISHING DEEP JUST BEFORE OR EARLY IN THE HATCH

SHALLOW NYMPH

IMITATION EMERGER OR DUN AT THE SURFACE DURING THE HATCH

The *Callibaetis* nymph is an agile swimmer; an imitation should appear to be also. But remember that "agile" in insect terms still means slow. In a lake with good hatches, the nymph is ever-present. So an imitation can always be trolled or cast on a sinking line (type III or type IV for trolling; type I or type II for casting) and worked shallow to deep.

Another approach includes a floating line, a long leader, patience, and a well-weighted fly. It's like the chironomid method, but quicker, though still almost painfully slow (see page 17).

Just before or at the beginning of a hatch, this same method works well—until the trout move to the top. After that, cast a dry fly, emerger, or lightweight nymph to where the trout are sipping. You can give the dry fly the tiniest twitch now and then, the same with the emerger; but tease the nymph slowly among the feeding trout.

HEXAGENIA

The *Hexagenia* mayfly is often called simply the "hex" (and in the Midwest, it's called the "Michigan Caddis," though it's clearly no caddisfly). The hex is an enormous nymph, then an enormous dun, and finally (of course) an enormous spinner. Imitations are tied on hooks no smaller than 8 and as large as 4—all 3X long. This species is found across North America, though its need for a certain composition of silt restricts it to a lake here, a lake there. But a lake with hexes is an angler's find, as hatches are often remarkably dense, which, combined with the size of this insect, tends to put the trout on hard attack. A hex hatch and the fishing it produces is seldom less than an event.

JIM SCHOLLMEYER

HEXAGENIA NYMPH

The full-grown *Hexagenia* nymph is thick and pale and yellow-brown with three fringed tails. It swims up from its hollow in the mud to hatch at the surface out in open water.

Some anglers fish an imitation along the bottom just before the hatch. At the start of the hatch, a nymph can be good, at the surface or down a few feet. But once everything is well under way, I nearly always fish a dry fly or emerger.

HEXAGENIA DUN

The *Hexagenia* dun is a dazzling bright-yellow and often comes off in dazzling numbers. The hatch can last just 20 minutes or up to two or three hours, and won't usually begin till the ghosts of sunset all but fade completely into night. On dark days it may begin sooner and spread itself thinly over hours. Though the body of the hatch usually lasts just two or three weeks, I've seen hatches that last a couple of months! It starts around mid to late summer. Spinners often return to the water before all the duns have escaped it, both mingling in their separate tasks on the lake's black face.

FISHING THE *HEXAGENIA* HATCH

When the hatch truly detonates, fish a dun or emerger. Make it twitch or tremble to suggest the adult squirming from its shuck and flexing its wings. Some anglers tease a nymph just under the surface. The spinner I've never found important. (See the illustration for fishing a mayfly hatch on page 46.)

Rick Hafele has heard of good fishing at night to the falling spinners. I can't say—the duns come off late enough for my tastes as it is.

SIPHLONURUS

Brian's lakes lack the *Siphlonurus* hatch, and I've never seen it. So I had a long talk with Jim Schollmeyer, the author of *Hatch Guide for Lakes*. Most of what follows came from him.

Siphlonurus and *Hexagenia* mayflies have much in common: Both are big (though the largest by far is the hex), both are rare (few lakes hold good numbers of either), and both usually hatch at dark in abundance. The big difference lies in the way they hatch. The hex (like most mayflies) swims up to hatch in the open while *Siphlonurus* creeps along the bottom to crawl out and hatch on whatever it finds at the lake's edges. *Siphlonurus* is big, as I said; imitations are tied on hooks 10 and 12.

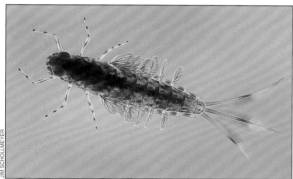
SIPHLONURUS NYMPH

The *Siphlonurus* nymph with its three fringed tails can be light-gray to dark-gray or yellow to tan. On the whole, the nymph is not important, except on occasion. Near hatching-time the nymphs can bring the trout to the shallows—just a couple of feet deep. That's when a nymph in the shallows worked briskly can pay off handsomely.

Since the *Siphlonurus* dun remains safe on shore in the brush and the trees, the trout seldom see it. The dun is shown here. It tends to hatch best in late spring to early summer, and in fall. But the spinner, not the dun, is what matters to trout and anglers. It goes to the water, just out from shore, releases its eggs, then lies sprawled upon the surface, trembling and dying. In some places, morning is the spinner's time; other places it's evening.

Fish *Siphlonurus* spinners as you would *Callibaetis*, but look for them not too far out from shore.

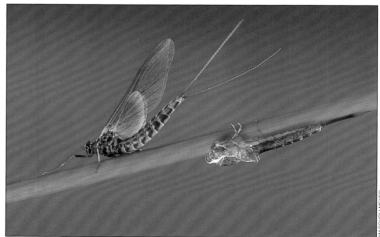
SIPHLONURUS DUN

TRICORYTHODES

Though Brian and I have both fished this hatch, we've done so too seldom to know it well. So I turned, a second time, to Jim Schollmeyer for help.

Tricorythodes has one outstanding feature—its size, which is tiny indeed. Hooks of size 20, 22, even 24 are used for making imitations. Most anglers just call these diminutive mayflies "tricos."

In lakes clear across North America, trico hatches are sparsely scattered. But where tricos live, they are often abundant, hatching daily for months, the spinners falling so close on the surface that tangled legs tie bodies into clusters.

JIM SCHOLLMEYER

TRICORYTHODES DUN

The nymph of *Tricorythodes* is private and tiny. Trout seldom see it or seek it.

The dun (shown here) is more promising. The males slip through their hatching at night, the dark and their size making them safe from predators. The females follow early the next morning; the light makes their risk much greater. Their hatching continues for two or three hours. And the trout feed upon them, but only in the absence of wind. July through September are this mayfly's hatching months.

FISHING THE *TRICORYTHODES* HATCH AND SPINNER FALL

The female duns begin hatching in the morning and soon, often before they are finished, the spinners arrive. It is best to imitate whichever form predominates, though with such tiny flies the trout will often take anything of proper size. Spinner falls can be immense.

Trout, though feeding, are often particular when trico spinners are falling. Perhaps with so many models for comparison nearby, trout tend to recognize an imposter. Or perhaps so tiny a fly is lost amid the copious specs and clots of miniscule insects. Whatever the reason, this is why some abandon the tricos in frustration while others, in fascination, take up their challenge.

Fish an emerger or imitation dun or spinner to the rises, still or perhaps with the tiniest twitches, as described for *Callibaetis*. But remember, your fly is but a spec—a trout won't go far to get it, and if it is far he probably won't see it. Judge the trout well. Anticipate. Cast true.

LLOYD HORWOOD

CADDISFLIES

The British and Canadians have long called them sedges; Americans call them caddisflies. They have a three-stage cycle of larva, pupa, adult. There are myriad species, too many to list and identify here, too many for me to want to. And a broad range of size—imitations for lake-caddis are tied on hooks of size-16 to -4. The colors of their bodies are as varied as their species and size—choose almost any color and a caddis will match it. Here are a few: green (caddis and green—always good), brown, yellow (these first three are the most common), ginger, gray, black, white. All these colors apply to both pupa and adult. The larva is another matter, as I'll explain next.

Most caddis larvae in lakes dwell within cases they build of sand or stones or twigs or bark or all of these or other things. This cumbersome case is fairly mobile, allowing the creature to get about. . . and into trouble. Trout consume case and all, but do so mostly early in spring or late in fall. But those larvae that are building new cases, having outgrown and cast off their old ones, exposed, soft, helpless, must surely be trout's favorites. The caseless larvae are usually pale, green, tan, or yellow, and are dark around the thorax.

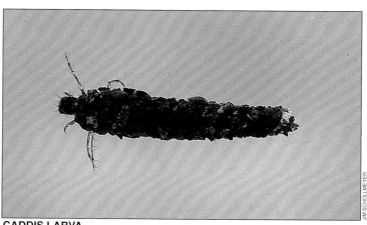

CADDIS LARVA

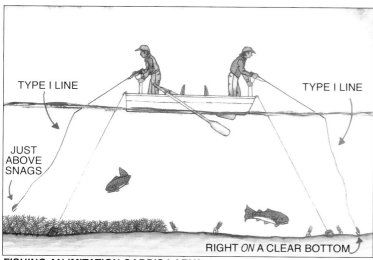

FISHING AN IMITATION CADDIS LARVA

Fishing an imitation caddis larva is no casual task. The fly must do as the pupa does—lumber along the bottom. Brian fishes an imitation (he prefers to imitate a caseless larva, naked in the building of its new case) slowly right on the bottom with a type I line—if the bottom is fairly free of snags. If the bottom wants to snag his fly, he fishes it just inches above the trouble, and the trout overlook the fact that caddis larvae do not hover. He concentrates his efforts at ten feet of depth or less, because that is where trout mostly feed in early spring and late fall, and when caddis larvae most often hold their attention.

Rising swiftly, stroking hard its paddlelike front legs, buoyed by gasses trapped within its swollen shuck, the caddis pupa seeks the surface, and there it hatches, provided trout don't interfere.

Depths to 20 feet, but usually less—sometimes fairly shallow—launch the hatching pupa. Caddis hatching comes mostly in summer and spring, although I've seen it as late as nearly winter. Time of day also varies, with so many caddis varieties of such varied habits.

CADDIS PUPA

ADULT CADDIS

Adult caddisflies all look similar to moths and similar to one another, their resting wings forming a sort of tent. Upon hatching, many caddisflies will stretch their new wings skyward and twist them up in the drying air, looking, briefly, quite like mayflies. Some caddisflies then dance, flitting and falling, trying to fly off. Others sprint, running and resting, trying to dry their wings.

The caddis adult shown here is the travelling sedge, the giant lake-caddis. Though it's distributed across North America, it's somewhat uncommon. Its name—"travelling"—comes from its marathon runs, wings folded, legs flicking in wild scramble.

Trout will sometimes swirl first at big caddis like this to take them under; the second swirl completes the job. Waiting to set the hook on the second swirl requires great restraint. A trait which can, if not inherited, be learned.

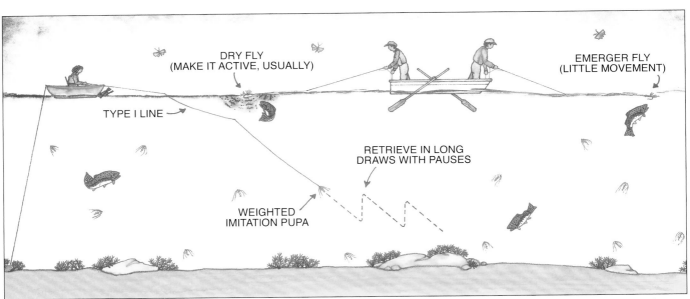

DRY FLY
(MAKE IT ACTIVE, USUALLY)

EMERGER FLY
(LITTLE MOVEMENT)

TYPE I LINE

RETRIEVE IN LONG
DRAWS WITH PAUSES

WEIGHTED
IMITATION PUPA

FISHING A CADDIS HATCH

During a caddis hatch, cast a well-weighted pupa and a type I full-sinking line (a floating line will do) and then allow it to sink. Retrieve the fly in long rapid draws ("rapid," that is, for a swimming insect), with a brief rest now and then.

If trout are rising, you may try an emerger-fly—cast it to risers and then leave it still, or move it slightly. But the standard offering for adult-caddis-chasing trout is a dry fly—watch the adults' behavior, and make your dry fly behave as they do.

Commonly, trout and anglers concentrate on adult caddis during a hatch, which can come off well out from shore if the depth there is right. But another time to fish a dry-fly caddis is when the adults fly to the water from lakeside trees, grasses, and brush to deposit their eggs or sip water (yes, they actually drink!). At these times, the action will be close to shore.

DAMSELFLIES

Tiny blue twigs flitting on wings—"blue bottles" my childhood friends and I called them. That name never made sense to me, because though they were indeed brilliant blue, they bore no similarity whatsoever to a bottle. "Damselflies" fly fishers call them, and that strikes me as reasonable—their delicate form and flight do seem feminine.

Damselflies are generously spread around this Earth. Their lives progress from nymph to adult. Though frail and slender, damsels are long—flies on hooks 2X or 3X long from 12 to 8 are common. That's big enough to interest big trout.

Damselfly nymphs run olive to brown with three plumes for tails. Their hourglass eyes complete the loose circle formed by their tiny claw-feet. They live among water plants down to 15 feet deep, hunting and often thriving—hatches can be too good, the angler's poor fly lost in a multitude of slender swimmers.

When they hatch in spring and summer, they swim like slow fish, up, then to shore or to stalks or stems—to anything they can climb out on. Their swim is shallow, within three feet of the surface.

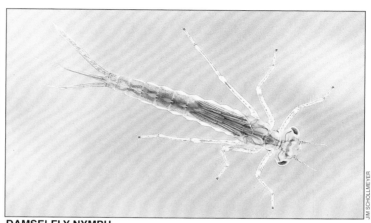

DAMSELFLY NYMPH

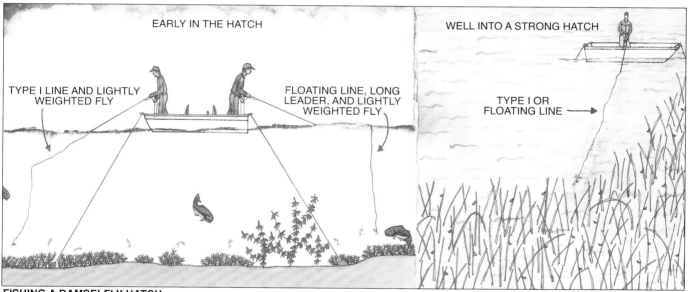

EARLY IN THE HATCH

WELL INTO A STRONG HATCH

TYPE I LINE AND LIGHTLY WEIGHTED FLY

FLOATING LINE, LONG LEADER, AND LIGHTLY WEIGHTED FLY

TYPE I OR FLOATING LINE →

FISHING A DAMSELFLY HATCH

In lakes rich with damsels, a damsel nymph on a sinking line is a fair choice any time from spring through fall. But hatch time, in such lakes, is an event.

At the very start of the daily hatch, when the damsel nymphs first begin ascending, Brian fishes a lightly weighted imitation slowly and deep, on a floating line and long leader or on a type I line and 9- to 12-foot leader.

Standard practice once the hatch is in full swing is to fish from the shallows, casting out, the fly swimming in. Give the fly a slow retrieve; pause it now and then. The likeliest places are near protruding plants—bulrushes, cattails, and such. Trout may swarm the shallows for damsels. They'll take them in water just knee-deep—or less. Signs of the damsel hatch include ragged shucks near the water, the nymphs sculling the surface, and damsel adults patrolling on wings.

A floating line is good, but seasoned damsel-fishers prefer a full-sinking type I.

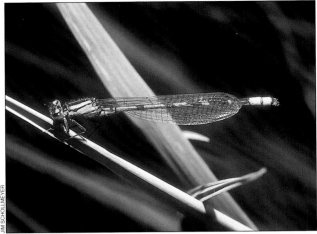

Male damsel adults are usually bright-blue in brilliant contrast to their hard-black markings. Fresh from the shuck they are pale olive, but that soon changes. Females are brown or tan. Adult damsels flutter gracefully yet boldly—they are quick to rest on the rod-tip.

In some places, at certain times, damselfly adults can interest trout, though Brian and I have seldom seen it. It can happen on a windy day, and the trout gather at the reeds and water plants to attack the tumbling adults. Toss your imitation in among the trapped and troubled; make it imitate their tussling and trembling.

DAMSELFLY ADULT

DRAGONFLIES

Their great size, more than anything else, makes dragonflies important, for their numbers are typically low. They are always fewer, for instance, than damselflies, with whom they share an ancient ancestry. Dragons seem to live wherever there is quiet fresh water. Their lives take the nymph-adult course. Libellulidae, one of the two main species, is often called Gomphidae, or Gomphus, but, Rick Hafele assures me, it is not.

The Libellulidae nymphs are long of leg, large and broad, spiderlike. They live atop silt, camouflaged by their flattened bodies and dull mottling. When prey happens by, these dragons strike with remarkable speed. Hooks for imitations run up to size-6.

Summer is when these dragonflies hatch. They creep—not swim—to the edges, then crawl out and slough off their shucks. They emerge from the water at night, but the active nymphs creeping shoreward can bring the trout searching all day long, especially since most of the other hatching things in the lake, by now, have hatched.

LIBELLULIDAE NYMPH

AESCHNIDAE NYMPH

In its nymphal stage, Aeschnidae (often called the "green darner") is huge, stout, and active. (Hooks for imitations run from long-shank 8 to long-shank 4.) While Libellulidae nymphs lie in wait for prey, Aeschnidae is out and aggressively hunting. Mainly, the Aeschnidae nymph lives around water plants and wood debris. It crawls to shore and then climbs out of the water to hatch, like Libellulidae.

AN IMITATION DRAGON NYMPH CAN BE GOOD ANY TIME, FISHED CLOSE TO THE BOTTOM

DURING THE HATCH, CAST FROM THE SHALLOWS OUT TO THE DEPTHS. WORK THE FLY CLOSE TO THE BOTTOM

FISHING AN IMITATION DRAGONFLY NYMPH

A dragon nymph fished any time from spring through fall, from the shallows to water as deep as a drop-off, can be productive. (Along a drop-off's edge is sometimes very good.) Work the fly near the bottom, on a sinking line (unless it's shallow), slowly or in darts or some of both.

The best time to fish a dragon nymph is hatch time. Then the real nymphs are on the move, exposing themselves along the way. The action is spread from mid-morning to almost evening. Work the fly along the bottom, slowly with maybe a lurch now and then, casting from the shallows out to the depths.

AN ADULT DRAGONFLY

Appearing like an inflated giant damselfly, the adult dragon is a swift, articulate flyer, buzzing the air in search of prey. Unlike all the other hatching insects here, the dragon adult lives long and feeds.

Trout, however, seldom feed upon it. Perhaps because they seldom get the chance. The dragon adult is a wonder, dazzling the angler with its swoops and hovers. But in 20 years on lakes, Brian has seen a dragon adult come from a trout's stomach only twice.

CREATURES TROUT EAT THAT DO NOT HATCH

WATER BOATMEN AND BACK SWIMMERS

Water boatmen are grazers; back swimmers hunt. Because grazers tend, in all forms of life, to be abundant while hunters tend to be few, boatmen will usually outnumber back swimmers by quite a margin. Of the two, the back swimmer is the slightly larger. But in all other ways that matter to fly fishers, and to trout, these two oar-leg swimmers are one. Shown here is the water boatman; the back swimmer is nearly a match. In hook-sizes 16 to 10, a single fly pattern can imitate both.

A WATER BOATMAN

Looking like plump tiny rowboats, water boatmen act something like them too, stroking like mad with their two oar-legs, swimming swiftly in rapid darts. They carry a glistening bubble of air on their belly, which feeds their breathing. Because they must refresh that air at intervals, they live no deeper than around four feet. This generally keeps them in the shallows or near the edges, among the water plants they choose as home.

All just said for the water boatman holds true for the back swimmer.

FISHING AN IMITATION WATER BOATMAN OR BACK SWIMMER

Water boatmen and back swimmers turn bold and active with their early spring mating. That is one time that trout seek them. In Brian's Kamloops lakes, ice-off finds boatmen and back swimmers in a frenzy, skittering across the surface, swimming wildly, buzzing briefly up into the air (yes, they fly—whenever they wish!), then diving back down under water again. In fall, after the first frosts warn them of winter, they fly from places grown too small or shallow, dropping at the glimmer of water. This is called the "boatman fall," when boatmen plop like raindrops onto nearly any part of a lake.

In spring, when boatmen and back swimmers celebrate their freedom from celibacy, a fast-sinking full-sinking line (type III or IV) and an unweighted fly can be deadly. Cast out and let the line sink a few feet among signs of feeding trout. Make a jerking, quick retrieve—the line pulls the fly into a dive, swings it down, and then up. All of which mimic the natural's course.

This approach also works well in the fall, when the insects plunk down on the surface. But after their crash, often they're stunned, quiet or twitching. A dry fly cast in the path of a trout and given a twitch now and then recreates this effect.

When the insects are wild and the trout feed with fury, I find that a fly fished just under the surface, neither diving nor rising, is as deadly as any.

Finally, in lakes thick with boatmen or back swimmers where trout stalk the shallows, a weighted fly cast ahead of their path, allowed to sink slightly, then worked past their nose can be deadly.

SCUDS

Often referred to as "freshwater shrimp," scuds are actually crustaceans. Sometimes gray or tan, they are usually green. Their size-range calls for flies on hooks size-18 to -8. There are two common genera of scuds, but they are so much alike in color, behavior, and form that I'll treat them as one. Scuds need water high in the calcium from which they form their shells, and are therefore scarce in water that is calcium-poor. Because productive lakes are often calcium-rich, many contain a heavy load of scuds, and in such lakes scuds usually account for the bulk of trout-pounds.

Scuds are constantly present and available throughout the year, and it's amazing how long trout can focus on them at a time. On Lac Le Jeune in Canada one spring, I found through pumping throats that trout fed mainly on scuds for weeks, shifting each midday to mayflies briefly. This was during a cold and blustery spring, after the chironomids had slowed and while the damsels and dragons awaited some warmth for their hatching.

Scuds never hatch. They just scurry and feed and grow and are eaten, all under water. They usually live around such cover as wood debris and water plants from only inches up to 25 feet deep. You'll see in the shallows, of lakes in which they thrive, scuds in their straight sprinting swims, following closely invisible lines that suddenly veer up or down, left or right. Poke around in the water, turn a rock, stir some plants—if the lake has good numbers of scuds, they'll appear. Expect scuds to be olive-green, sometimes gray, occasionally orange.

SCUD

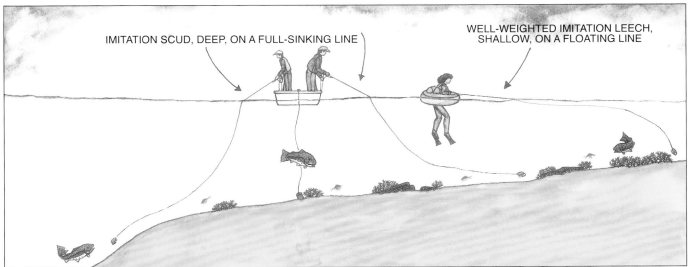

IMITATION SCUD, DEEP, ON A FULL-SINKING LINE

WELL-WEIGHTED IMITATION LEECH, SHALLOW, ON A FLOATING LINE

FISHING AN IMITATION SCUD

The heaviest feeding of trout on scuds comes in spring and fall, when little else is active and out. Scuds are erratic swimmers, so fish a scud-fly slowly, near the bottom, with pauses.

Brian will fish a well-weighted imitation scud, slowly on a floating line and long leader, from shallow water down to 20 feet deep.

On full-sinking lines, from type I to type III depending on depth, a scud can be trolled or cast over drop-offs or shoals, around water plants, or up in shallows—any place, in fact, where scuds live, which means anywhere at all in a lake save its greater depths.

LEECHES

Raising and dipping its hideous sleek head sending swimming waves down its wormy form, the leech prowls the bed of a lake, scavenging and hunting. Most leech species feed upon insects and such and on flesh they find that's already dead; a few suck blood from amphibians and fishes; only a very few will attach to humans (which, though reassuring, hardly constitutes a virtue). Perhaps their most offensive feature is having a sucker at each end, or perhaps it's that they can draw up their bodies into lumpy bulbs of goo.

I hate the sight of leeches, I hate the squishy feel of leeches, I hate the fleshy swim of leeches, and the fact that trout eat leeches doesn't improve the status of leeches in my opinion; it only lowers the status of trout.

LEECH

Most full-grown leeches are about four-inches long. Leeches are brown or black or olive or tan and sometimes spotted. (None of these colors improves their looks.) They swim and slither in shallows and depths. In daylight they are usually hidden, unless some feeding opportunity like a chironomid hatch draws them out. Night is normally when they are out and prowling. (If you were a leech, would you show your face in the light?)

WELL-WEIGHTED IMITATION LEECH, SHALLOW, ON A FLOATING LINE

IMITATION LEECH DEEP ON A FULL-SINKING LINE

FISHING AN IMITATION LEECH

Generally leech flies are best in spring, mid- to late-summer, and late fall. Brian believes it's the chironomid hatches that bring leeches out in the daylight of spring. Later, in summer, the scarcity of other things trout eat makes leeches stand out, as it does again in late fall. Leech imitations are good for fishing at night, because that's when real leeches prowl.

Leech flies are common in trolling. They can also be cast on sinking lines. Work them in slowly, just off the bottom, in pulses. Nearly any depth can be good, but the mid-depths are usually best. Sometimes in water not too deep, with a well-weighted leech fly, Brian fishes a floating line with a long leader and works it all with particular slowness.

TERRESTRIALS

Though most insects whose lives are meant for the land seldom end up in water, there are many exceptions which can be important. Flying ants, for example, have provided me fine fishing on lakes many times, flitting out and dropping onto a lake, ants of different sizes and colors at all times of day and seemingly any time from early spring through fall. And I've heard from solid sources of grasshoppers taken by breezes to the waiting mouths of trout in lakes. In lakes whose edges are shaded by branches and littered with half-submerged logs, shallow trout sometimes seem to be hunting terrestrials—ants, beetles, spiders, and such. But because such trout are usually taking whatever they find, close imitation in a fly may be unnecessary.

Flying ants are usually red, black, or brown. Their size varies widely—hooks for imitations range from 22 to 8, with 12 as typical. Different ants show up at different times of day and season; I've seen ants out and trout in pursuit from early spring through fall, in morning, afternoon, and at dusk. The only common factor I've found among all the species is that hot days usually encourage ants to fly, and, therefore, to fall into lakes.

A FLYING ANT

I've often heard the theory about ants being too acidic for trout to feed upon them beyond a day or two. But Rick Hafele assures me that trout will often stay on ants just as long as the supply is ample.

To fish a flying-ant fly, just toss it out among the naturals, where the trout are showing, and make it twitch or rest depending on the natural's behavior.

MISCELLANEOUS

The trout-food creatures we've covered thus far are the standard lake-assortment; you will encounter them time and again in trout lakes across North America, and throughout the world.

But keep your eyes alert and your brain unchecked—no book or chapter can deal with every whim of trout and Nature. In some lakes or regions, you may find water beetles, alderflies, tiny fishes, crayfish, or other varied creatures in abundance, and find the trout set strictly onto them. Regardless of how much you read, how much you fish, how much you learn, there will always be surprises. Always. And wouldn't it all become dull if there weren't?

RETRIEVES FOR IMITATIONS

Brian has fished, for more than two decades, season after season, to trout that were feeding on each of the creatures we've explored in this chapter. And for more than two decades he's studied those creatures and how they move, in order to recreate that movement in his flies. The retrieves described on the next page were carefully honed by slow degrees, by a long process of observation and trial-and-error. They deserve careful practice with a timepiece. Truth is, most anglers jerk in their flies far more quickly than they realize, far more quickly than they should, and far more quickly than trout will forgive.

A complete hand-twist retrieve, from one thumb-and-finger pinch to the next, takes up exactly seven inches of fly line in Brian's hand. If your hand is significantly smaller or larger than an average man's, you might adjust your retrieves, slightly, against those on the next page.

Most dry-fly retrieves are plain enough and so inconstant that most details are pointless. But those few details that are useful are here.

You will often be told here to use the "count down"—which is explained in Chapter 3, "Fishing the Depths," on page 15.

CHIRONOMIDS

1. Imitation Chironomid Larva on a Floating Line:

Six to 8 seconds for each full hand-twist; give several quick 2- to 3-inch draws every 25 to 35 seconds.

2. Imitation Chironomid Pupa Well Down on a Floating Line:

In a breeze, no retrieve until the line is straight downwind; then 4 to 8 seconds for each full hand-twist, every 35 to 40 seconds a quick 2- to 3-inch draw or two, occasional pauses of up to 10 to 20 seconds.

3. Imitation Chironomid Pupa Straight Down on a Type III Full-Sinking Line:

After the line is given enough time to hang straight down, use the retrieve just described for the "Imitation Chironomid Pupa Well Down on a Floating Line." Retrieve well up the leader for long-following trout.

MAYFLIES

4. Imitation *Callibaetis* Nymph on a Type I or II (Brian prefers a type I; I prefer a type II) Full-Sinking Line:

Three seconds for each full hand-twist, with 2 or 3 quick 3-inch strips every 15 to 20 seconds.

5. Well-Weighted Imitation *Callibaetis* Nymph on a Floating Line:

After counting down, 4 seconds for each full hand-twist with 2 or 3 quick 3-inch strips occasionally. Start with the nymph just off the bottom and then work it higher and higher until you find trout.

CADDISFLIES

6. Unweighted Imitation Caddis Larva on a Type I Full-Sinking Line:

Use the count down to get the fly just off the bottom; then 2 seconds for each full hand-twist, occasional quick 2- to 3-inch strips.

7. Well-Weighted Imitation Caddis Pupa on a Type I Full-Sinking Line:

Use the count down to get the fly just off the bottom, then the following retrieve should swing it steadily upwards: 4- to 8-inch steady strips of moderate speed, several quick 2- to 3-inch strips every 30 to 40 seconds.

8. Well-Weighted Imitation Caddis Pupa on a Floating Line:

The same retrieve as just described for the type I line, but vary the count down to start the fly ascending from different depths, until the most productive starting-depth emerges.

9. Imitation Adult Travelling Sedge on a Floating Line:

Quick 4- to 8-inch strips with an occasional pause of 1 to 3 seconds.

DAMSELFLIES

10. Imitation Damselfly Nymph on a Type I Full-Sinking or a Floating Line:

Let the fly drop to about three feet down, then medium-slow partial hand-twists of 2 to 4 inches of line, occasional 2- or 3-second pauses

11. Well-Weighted Imitation Damselfly Nymph Down on a Floating Line (for fishing to trout taking deeper nymphs):

Use the count down to get the fly near the bottom; then 2 seconds for each full hand-twist. The fly should steadily rise.

DRAGONFLIES

12. Imitation Libellulidae Dragonfly Nymph on a Type I or II Full-Sinking Line:

Use the count down to put the fly near the bottom, then 2 seconds for each hand-twist with several quick 2- to 3-inch strips occasionally.

13. Imitation Aeshnidae Dragonfly Nymph on a Type II Full-Sinking Line:

Use the count down to put the fly near the bottom, then moderate-slow 3- to 8-inch strips with several quick 2- to 3-inch strips occasionally.

WATER BOATMEN AND BACK SWIMMERS

14. Imitation Adult Water Boatmen on a Type III or IV Full-Sinking Line (not a "uniform-sink" line, a conventional line that will sink in a curve):

Fast 3- to 4-inch strips. The line should draw the fly down and then swing it back up. (Sometimes it's perfectly effective to keep the fly just under the surface with a type I, same retrieve.)

SCUDS

15. Well-Weighted Imitation Scud on a Floating Line in up to 20 feet of water:

Use the count down to put the fly near the bottom; then 2 to 3 seconds for each full hand-twist, a few quick 3- to 6-inch strips after every three hand-twists or so.

16. Imitation Scud on a Type I Full-Sinking Line:

Simply speed up slightly the retrieve described above for an imitation scud on a floating line.

LEECHES

17. Well-Weighted Imitation Leech in 6 Feet or less of Depth on a Floating Line:

Two seconds for a full hand-twist, mixed with quick strips. For night fishing, triple the speed of the retrieve.

18. Imitation Leech on a Type I or Type II Full-Sinking Line (25 to 35 feet deep):

Let the line settle straight down; then 3 to 4 seconds for each full hand-twist, occasional short, quick strips.

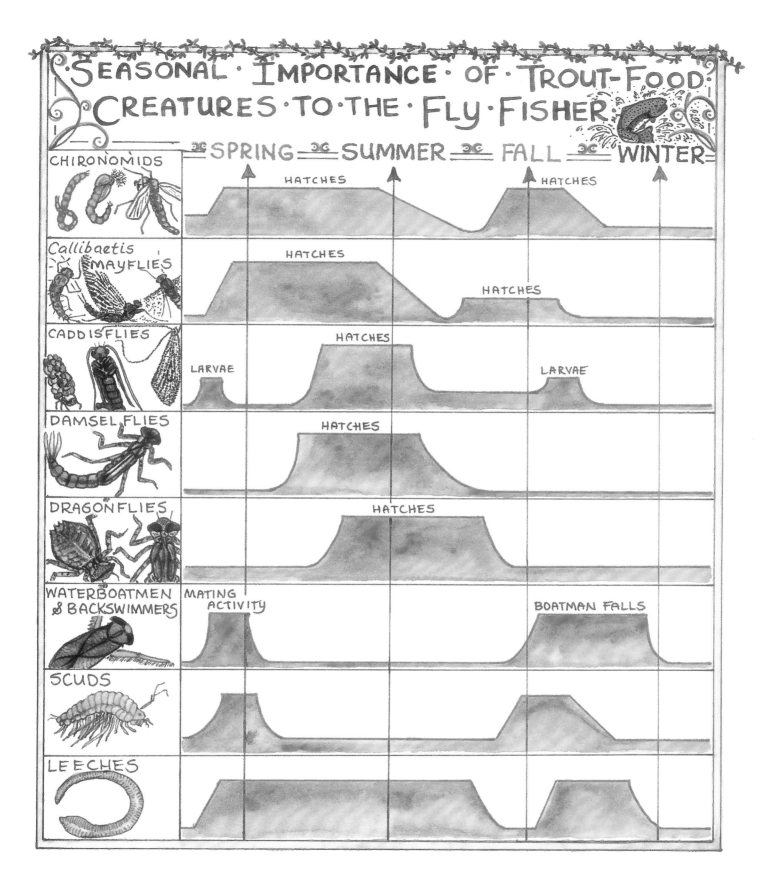

SEASONAL · IMPORTANCE · OF · TROUT-FOOD · CREATURES · TO · THE · FLY · FISHER

SPRING — SUMMER — FALL — WINTER

CHIRONOMIDS — HATCHES — HATCHES

Callibaetis MAYFLIES — HATCHES — HATCHES

CADDISFLIES — LARVAE — HATCHES — LARVAE

DAMSEL FLIES — HATCHES

DRAGONFLIES — HATCHES

WATERBOATMEN & BACKSWIMMERS — MATING ACTIVITY — BOATMAN FALLS

SCUDS

LEECHES

8

FLIES FOR TROUT LAKES

The most important factor in making a fly an effective imitation of a particular insect (or other creature trout eat) is *movement*—the fly must appear to swim, lie still, or struggle as the real insect does. Second in importance is its *size*—the fly must be the same length as the insect. Third in importance is *form*—primarily, the fly should suggest the overall outline of the insect, and to a lesser degree, mimic wings, tails, legs and other details. Fourth is *shade*—regardless of color, the fly should match the overall lightness or darkness of the natural. The fifth and last (which beginning anglers often put first) is actual *color*.

So, exactly matching a particular chironomid pupa's gray-green abdomen and mahogany thorax doesn't mean much if the fly is half again as long as the natural, or darts across the bottom while the real pupa just drifts slowly upwards and wriggles a little now and then.

That, at least, is how Brian and I see the matter of making imitative flies effective, and lots of experienced fly fishers see it the same way.

The fact that we've presented five criteria for matching flies to naturals may make the task seem complicated, but really, it isn't. From the previous chapters on fishing techniques and the chapter on the creatures trout eat in lakes, you know how to make a fly behave like a number of natural trout foods. Your new knowledge about those creatures, combined with catching and inspecting a sample if possible, will make selecting a good fly and fishing it effectively a fairly straightforward operation.

Besides, only the fussiest of trout require just the right fly fished just the right way—most of the time, if the fly and retrieve are somewhere in the ballpark, you're catching fish.

Consequently, Brian and I believe that a small selection of fly patterns will catch trout in lakes with good consistency. The subject below, "A Beginning Selection of Flies" describes just such a selection. But following that are forty excellent fly patterns you can rely on for trout lakes again and again—add these to your fly boxes and you'll really be prepared.

No collection of fly patterns, though, no matter how extensive, can cover every possible lake-fishing situation. So expect to add new fly patterns as you continue fishing lakes.

A BEGINNING SELECTION OF FLIES

The short list below is a minimal selection of flies for lakes, but you'll be surprised at how often it works. Within the list is one set of fly patterns for the fly tier, and another set for the fly purchaser. We wanted to include fly tiers of all skill levels, so we chose for them simple fly patterns that were easy to tie. And for the fly buyer we chose patterns that are commonly available in fly shops and catalogues, and included alternates just in case.

Our advice: start with three—or at least, two—flies of each pattern from your tier's or purchaser's set.

FOR CHIRONOMIDS

BUYER'S PATTERN: TDC
TIER'S PATTERN: TDC
SIZE: 14
ALTERNATE BUYER'S PATTERNS: Chan's Frostbite Chironomid Pupa, Brassie

FOR MAYFLIES (*CALLIBAETIS* ONLY)

BUYER'S PATTERNS: Gold Ribbed Hare's Ear, Parachute Adams
TIER'S PATTERNS: Skip Nymph, Olive Sparkle Dun
SIZE: 14
ALTERNATE BUYER'S PATTERN:
Nymphs: Pheasant Tail, Skip Nymph
Dry Flies: Olive Comparadun, Olive Sparkle Dun, Olive Thorax Dun

FOR CADDISFLIES

BUYER'S PATTERNS: Brown Sparkle Pupa, Elk Hair Caddis
TIER'S PATTERNS: Bead Head Caddis Pupa, Olive; Elk Hair Caddis
SIZE: 12
ALTERNATE BUYER'S PATTERNS:
Nymphs: Halfback, Bird's Nest, Zug Bug

FOR DAMSELFLIES

BUYER'S PATTERN: Every fly shop and mail-order house seems to have its own damsel-nymph imitation. Nearly all are effective when fished well—Brian and I suggest you take what they offer
TIER'S PATTERN: Halfback
SIZE: 10 (2X or 3X long hook)

FOR DRAGONFLIES

BUYER'S PATTERN: Olive Woolly Bugger. (Dave Hughes suggests you pinch and tear the tail to half its original length, and I agree)
TIER'S PATTERN: Carey Special
SIZE: 8 (2X or 3X long hook)
ALTERNATE BUYER'S PATTERNS: Carey Special, Brown Woolly Bugger (again, tear the tail), Doc Spratley

FOR WATER BOATMEN, BACK SWIMMERS

BUYER'S PATTERN: Zug Bug
TIER'S PATTERN: Simple Water Boatman
SIZE: 12
ALTERNATE BUYER'S PATTERNS: Prince Nymph. Another choice: whatever your fly shop or mail-order house offers as an imitation

FOR SCUDS

BUYER'S PATTERN: Any plastic-sheet-back imitation your fly shop or mail-order house offers
TIER'S PATTERN: Scud
SIZE: 12
ALTERNATE BUYER'S PATTERNS: Zug Bug. Another choice: any back-swimmer or water-boatman imitation (trim off the oar-legs, if you wish)

FOR LEECHES

BUYER'S PATTERN: Black Woolly Bugger
TIER'S PATTERN: Black Woolly Bugger
SIZE: 6 (2X or 3X long hook)
ALTERNATE BUYER'S PATTERNS: Brown Woolly Bugger, Bead-Head Woolly Bugger (black or brown), Black Marabou Leech

FOR TERRESTRIALS

BUYER'S PATTERN: Black Flying Ant (sometimes called Flying Black Ant)
TIER'S PATTERN: Ant Carol (brown)
SIZE: 12
ALTERNATE BUYER'S PATTERNS: Black Fur Ant, Black Foam Ant

CHIRONOMID IMITATIONS

FOR IMITATING LARVAE

KAMLOOPS BLOODWORM

Brian Chan (tied by Brian)
Hook: Heavy wire, 3X long, sizes 14 to 10.
Thread: Eight-ought or 6/0 in the body's color.
Tail: A small bunch of marabou fibers to match the body's color.
Rib: Fine copper or silver wire.
Body: One strand of red (for the bloodworm), olive-green, tan, or light-brown Super Floss or Flexi Floss.
RETRIEVES: #1 (page 58). Also, it can be cast to risers and fished barely submerged and barely jiggled around turnover time.

FOR IMITATING PUPAE

CHAN'S CHIRONOMID

Brian Chan (tied by Brian)
Hook: Heavy wire, 2X long, sizes 14 and 12.
Thread: Brown 8/0 or 6/0.
Tail: White poly yarn.
Rib: Fine copper wire.
Abdomen: Pheasant-tail fibers.
Wing Case: Pheasant-tail fibers.
Thorax: Peacock herl.
Gills: White Antron fibers bound crossways, short.
RETRIEVES: #2 and #3 (page 58).

CHAN'S FROSTBITE CHIRONOMID PUPA

Brian Chan (tied by Brian)
Hook: Heavy wire, standard length (humped shank is optional), sizes 16 to 12.
Gills: A small bunch of white Antron yarn projecting off the hook's eye, from under the bead.
Thread: Black 8/0 or 6/0.
Bead: Copper bead, 1/8-inch diameter.
Rib: Fine silver wire.
Abdomen: Two strands of red, black, or chocolate brown Frostbite, unraveled from the main weave, or two strands of Krystal Flash, same colors.
Thorax: Peacock herl.
RETRIEVES: #2 and #3 (page 58).

TDC

Richard Thompson (tied by Skip)
Hook: Heavy wire, 1X long, sizes 18 to 8.
Thread: Black 6/0 or 8/0.
Rib: Narrow flat or oval silver tinsel.
Abdomen: Black (or another chironomid color) wool yarn or dubbed fur (I prefer rabbit).
Thorax: Fine chenille or dubbing in the abdomen's color.
Gills: White ostrich herl (I like to spin it around the thread for durability).
RETRIEVES: #2 and #3 (page 58). It can also be fished just under the surface, with occasional jiggles, to rising trout.

SKIP'S ICED CHIRONOMID

Skip Morris (tied by Skip)
Hook: Heavy wire, 1X long (humped shank is optional), sizes 10 and 8.
Bead: Black metal, 1/8" diameter.
Thread: 8/0 or 6/0 of the abdomen's color.
Tail: White Antron yarn, short.
Outer Abdomen: A gape-wide strip of clear plastic, as from a heavy plastic bag, bound at the hook's bend and pulled forward over the dubbed abdomen.
Rib: Black size-A rod-winding thread (or copper wire, tinsel, monofilament—whatever).
Inner Abdomen: Black, dark-green, medium-green, orange, or maroon Antron, dubbed.
Wing Case: A strip of the same plastic used over the abdomen, but only half as wide.
Thorax: Hare's mask or squirrel dubbed against the front of the bead, black with a black abdomen, dark brown with all others.
Gills: White Antron yarn bound crossways, short.
RETRIEVES: #2 and #3 (page 58).
COMMENTS: The Skip's Iced Chironomid imitates a huge chironomid pupa, which Canadians call a "bomber."

FOR IMITATING HATCHING ADULTS

GRIFFITH'S GNAT

George Griffith (tied by Skip)
Hook: Light wire, regular length to 1X long (standard dry-fly hook), sizes 18 to 8.
Thread: Black or olive 6/0 or 8/0.
Hackle: One, grizzly, palmered up the body.
Body: Peacock herl.
RETRIEVES: See "Lady McConnell," below.
COMMENTS: The Griffith's Gnat suggests the tangle of shuck and wings and body and legs that is a real hatching chironomid.

LADY McCONNELL

Brian Chan (tied by Brian)
Hook: Light wire, size-16 standard length to size-12 2X long.
Thread: Black 8/0 or 6/0.
Shuck: One grizzly hackle tip atop Z-lon.
Back: Natural deer hair, as a hump.
Body: The working thread.
Hackle: One, brown, trimmed flat beneath.
RETRIEVES: Cast it to trout that are seeking chironomids hatching at the surface; then move it very little, if at all.

MAYFLY IMITATIONS

FOR IMITATING NYMPHS

BURK'S HEXAGENIA

Andy Burk (tied by Skip)
Hook: Heavy wire, 2X or 3X long, sizes 8 to 4.
Weight: Lead wire over the thorax area.
Thread: Yellow 8/0, 6/0, or 3/0.
Tail: Natural gray marabou.
Back: Dark, mottled turkey-quill or turkey-tail section.
Rib: Fine copper wire.
Gills: Natural-gray filoplume pheasant feather, flat over the dubbing and under the turkey-back and rib.
Abdomen: Pale-yellow rabbit fur, dubbed.
Wing Case: Dark, mottled turkey-quill or turkey-tail section.
Thorax: Pale-yellow rabbit fur, dubbed.
Legs: Mottled brown hen saddle, a few turns drawn down and bound as a half-circle beard hackle.
RETRIEVES: Fish it deep or near the surface as described in Chapter 7 (page 46), in the section on the *Hexagenia* mayfly.

LEAD BELLY SKIP NYMPH, *CALLIBAETIS*

Skip Morris (tied by Skip)
Hook: Heavy wire, 1X long, sizes 16 to 12.
Bead: Size-14 hooks and smaller: 3/32-inch diameter, black-metal. Size-12: 1/8-inch diameter, black-metal.
Thread: Brown 8/0 or 6/0.
Rib: Fine copper wire.
Tails, Back, and Wing Case: Pheasant-tail fibers. I soak epoxy *glue* (not *finish*) into the wing case. Hot air from a hair dryer helps the epoxy flow.
Abdomen: Hare's mask or similarly colored squirrel, dubbed.
Thorax: The same dubbing used in the abdomen.
RETRIEVES: #5 (page 58).
COMMENTS: I also tie and fish this Lead Belly version in the darker colors of the Skip Nymph Dark and in the style of my Sparkle Skip Nymph.

SKIP NYMPH (STANDARD), *CALLIBAETIS*

Skip Morris (tied by Skip)
Hook: Heavy wire, 1X long, sizes 16 to 12.
Thread: Brown 8/0 or 6/0.
Rib and Weight: Fine copper wire.
Tails, Back, and Wing Case: Pheasant-tail fibers.
Abdomen: Hare's mask or squirrel of similar color.
Thorax: The same dubbing used in the abdomen.
RETRIEVES: #4 and (if well-weighted with lead or lead-substitute wire) #5 (page 58). Also, cast it to surface-feeding trout during the hatch.
COMMENTS: This remains my first choice for an imitation of the *Callibaetis* mayfly nymph—it's Brian's first choice, too.

We prefer the dark version (dark-brown dubbing and pheasant) when the trout aren't fussy.

Neither Brian nor I have fished the *Siphlonurus* mayfly hatch, so I can only guess that a size-10 or -12 Skip Nymph would be a good match, but with *gray* dubbing, it seems a sure bet.

SPARKLE SKIP NYMPH, *CALLIBAETIS*

Skip Morris (tied by Skip)
Hook: Heavy wire, 1X long, sizes 16 to 12.
Thread: Brown 8/0 or 6/0.
Rib and Weight: Fine copper wire.
Tails, Back, and Wing Case: Natural pheasant-tail fibers; topped with two strands of brownish Flashabou or Krystal Flash.
Abdomen: Hare's mask or similarly colored squirrel, hand-mixed with brown (any brownish color), pearl, and silver Flashabou Dubbing or Lite Brite.
Thorax: Just more of the abdomen's dubbing.
RETRIEVES: See "Skip Nymph (standard) *Callibaetis*" earlier in this chapter—same retrieves.
COMMENTS: Suggests the real nymph ripe for hatching, its shuck bright from the gasses trapped within and clinging as bubbles without.

FOR IMITATING HATCHING ADULTS

SPECKLED SPINNER SPARKLE DUN

Craig Mathews, John Juracek (tied by Skip)
Hook: Light wire, standard length to 1X long (standard dry-fly hook), sizes 16 to 12.
Thread: Tan 8/0 or 6/0.
Wing: Natural-brown, coastal deer hair.
Shuck: Olive-brown (I use brown) Z-lon or sparkle poly yarn, about one-half the shank's length.
Body: Tan dubbing.
RETRIEVES: Cast it to trout feeding on mayfly duns during a hatch; then give it an occasional tiny twitch.
COMMENTS: An imitation of a *Callibaetis* dun half-hatched or fatally tangled in its shuck. The name "Speckled Spinner Sparkle Dun" is itself nearly a fatal tangle.

FOR IMITATING DUNS

BUNSE HEX DUN

Richard Bunse (tied by Skip)
Hook: Light wire, short shank, sizes 8 and 6.
Thread: Yellow 8/0, 6/0, or 3/0.
Body: Ethafoam sheeting (a bubbly packing foam) 3/32-inch thick, colored with a yellow marking pen and coated with highly thinned Dave's Flexament.
Tails: Two mink-tail, nutria, or beaver guard hairs or pale Micro Fibetts.
Wing: Bleached coastal deer hair or bleached elk.
RETRIEVES: Fish it still or with occasional twitches during a *Hexagenia* mayfly hatch.
COMMENTS: I describe in detail the unusual tying of this unusual fly in two books: *The Art of Tying the Dry Fly* and *Tying Foam Flies*.

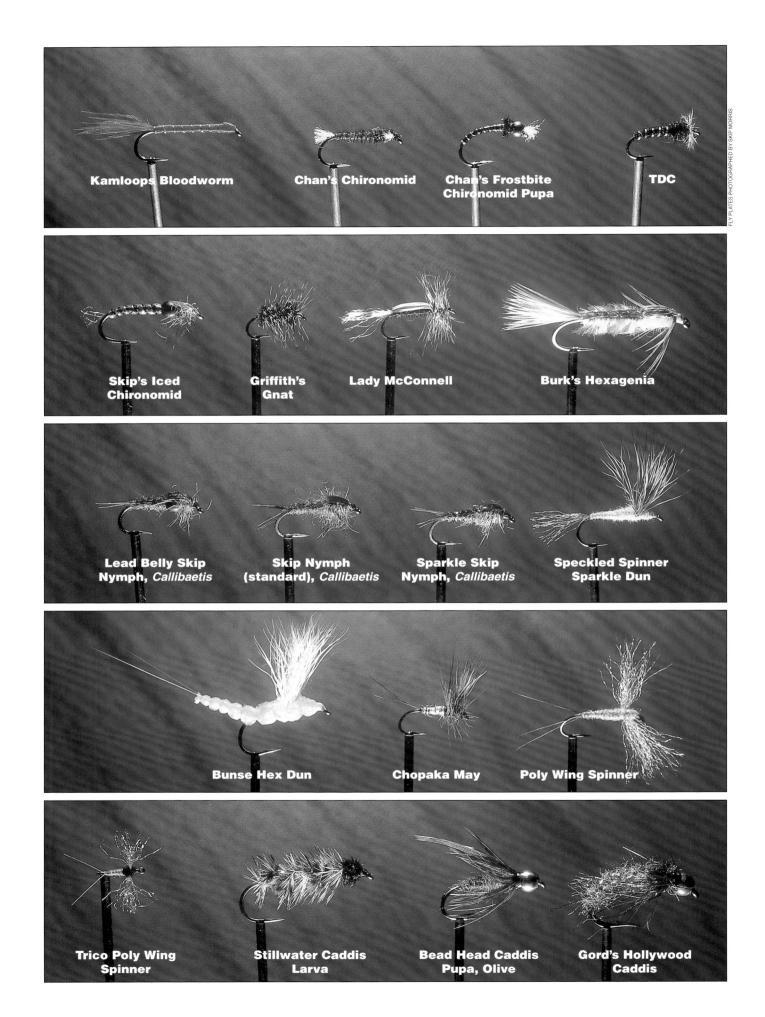

Kamloops Bloodworm

Chan's Chironomid

Chan's Frostbite Chironomid Pupa

TDC

Skip's Iced Chironomid

Griffith's Gnat

Lady McConnell

Burk's Hexagenia

Lead Belly Skip Nymph, *Callibaetis*

Skip Nymph (standard), *Callibaetis*

Sparkle Skip Nymph, *Callibaetis*

Speckled Spinner Sparkle Dun

Bunse Hex Dun

Chopaka May

Poly Wing Spinner

Trico Poly Wing Spinner

Stillwater Caddis Larva

Bead Head Caddis Pupa, Olive

Gord's Hollywood Caddis

CHOPAKA MAY

Boyd Aigner (tied by Brian)

Hook: Light wire, standard length to 1X long (standard dry-fly hook), sizes 16 to 10.
Thread: Black 8/0 or 6/0.
Tail: Two black bear hairs. (Substitutes could include a few black calf-tail or buck-tail hairs.)
Body: A few strands of gray sparkle yarn, or synthetic dubbing.
Wing: A single bunch of deer hair.
Hackle: One, blue dun, trimmed underneath to about even with the hook's point.
RETRIEVES: Fish it still or with occasional tiny twitches to trout feeding on a *Callibaetis* mayfly hatch.
COMMENTS: Time-tested and well-established in the Pacific Northwest for matching *Callibaetis* mayfly duns.

FOR IMITATING SPINNERS

POLY WING SPINNER

(tied by Skip)

Hook: Light wire, standard length to 1X long (standard dry-fly hook), sizes 16 to 10 for *Callibaetis*, 12 to 8 for *Siphlonurus.*
Thread: Eight-ought or 6/0 in a color to blend with the thorax.
Tails: Hackle fibers, split, blue-dun or gray for both *Callibaetis* and *Siphlonurus.*
Body: Synthetic dubbing, medium-gray for *Callibaetis*, brownish-gray for *Siphlonurus.*
Wing: A single length of gray (some prefer white) poly yarn or Antron yarn bound crossways.
RETRIEVES: Cast it to trout feeding on mayfly spinners, then move it *very* little, if at all.

TRICO POLY WING SPINNER

(tied by Skip)

Hook: Light wire, standard length, sizes 24 to 20.
Thread: Olive 8/0 or finer.
Tails: White hackle fibers, split.
Wings: White poly yarn.
Abdomen: Fine olive synthetic dubbing.
Thorax: Fine black synthetic dubbing.
RETRIEVES: Cast it to surface-feeding trout during hatches of the mayfly *Tricorythodes*; then leave it still.
COMMENTS: This fly represents the female; the male isn't so colorful: all black. Both colorings are productive.

CADDISFLY IMITATIONS

FOR IMITATING LARVAE

STILLWATER CADDIS LARVA

Brian Chan (tied by Brian)

Hook: Heavy wire, 2X long, sizes 12, 10, and 8.
Thread: Green or Olive 8/0 or 6/0.
Weight: Wrappings of lead or lead-substitute wire.
Rib: One grizzly hackle, its fibers trimmed short.
Sides: Two strands of pearlescent Flashabou pulled forward along each side of the abdomen and wrapped over with the rib.
Abdomen: Fine variegated chenille in yellow and green or olive and dark-green.
Thorax: Peacock herl (spun around the thread).
RETRIEVES: #6 (page 58).

FOR IMITATING PUPAE

BEAD HEAD CADDIS PUPA, OLIVE

(tied by Skip)

Hook: Heavy wire, 1X or 2X long, sizes 14 to 8.
Thread: Olive 8/0 or 6/0.
Bead: Gold (brass), size appropriate to hook-size.
Body: Olive rabbit fur, thick. Other standard colors include cream, brown, dark-gray.
Hackles: One mottled-brown hen-saddle hackle, one to two turns.
Antennae: Longer hen-saddle fibers, atop the hook. (Why not pheasant-tail fibers, or omit the antennae altogether?)
RETRIEVES: #7 and #8 (page 58).
COMMENTS: You have a tacit pact with me and Brian: You listen, we'll tell you the truth. So, truth is, though Brian and I haven't fished this *exact* pattern, we agree that it *must* be effective.

GORD'S HOLLYWOOD CADDIS

Gordon Honey (tied by Gordon Honey)

Hook: Heavy wire, short curved shank, sizes 10 to 6.
Bead: Copper or brass, 1/8-inch diameter for size 10 and 8 hooks, 5/32-inch for size 6.
Thread: Black 8/0, 6/0, or 3/0.
Rib: A single strand of yellow floss or flat waxed nylon, or medium-thick copper wire.
Abdomen: Dubbing (synthetic or natural) of various shades of green or rust.
Thorax, Wing Pads, Legs, and Antennae: Bronze (they call it "pheasant tail") Angel Hair, or bronze Flashabou Dubbing or Lite Brite. Trim the fibers to suggest thorax, wing pads (at the sides), legs, and long antennae.
RETRIEVES: #7 and #8 (page 58).

STILLWATER CADDIS PUPA

Brian Chan (tied by Brian)

Hook: Heavy wire, 2X or 3X long, sizes 12 to 8.
Thread: Brown 8/0 or 6/0.
Weight: Wrappings of lead or lead-substitute wire.
Rib: Lime-green Flexi Floss or Super Floss.
Abdomen: A mix of bronze, medium-green, and golden Arizona Synthetic dubbing (or some other shiny dubbing).
Wing Case: Pheasant-tail fibers.
Thorax: The same dubbing used in the abdomen.
Legs: Pheasant tail, six to eight fibers on each side.
Throat: Peacock-color Angel Hair.
Head: Peacock herl (twisted with the thread).
RETRIEVES: # 7 and #8 (page 58).

FOR IMITATING HATCHING ADULTS

B.C. CADDIS EMERGER

Brian Chan (tied by Brian)

Hook: Light wire, 2X long, sizes 12 to 8.
Thread: Eight-ought or 6/0 in the body's color.
Shuck: White Z-lon.
Rib: Super Floss or Flexi Floss (usually a lighter shade of the abdomen's color).
Abdomen: Tan, brown, bright- or olive-green synthetic dubbing. (Brian uses a dubbing loop.)
Wing and Hump: Natural deer hair, bound at the front of the abdomen and the front of the thorax.
Thorax: The same dubbing used in the abdomen, but without the rib.
Hackle: One, pale-brown.
Head: The butts of the wing-hump.
RETRIEVES: Fish it mostly dead still, a slow six- to eight-inch draw now and then.
COMMENTS: This fly represents a half-hatched caddis. A lime-green rib and bright-medium-green body on a size-8 or -10 hook imitates the travelling sedge. Other sizes and colors mimic other caddis.

FOR IMITATING ADULTS

ELK HAIR CADDIS

Al Troth (tied by Skip)

Hook: Light wire, standard length to 1X long (standard dry-fly hook), sizes 14 to 10.
Thread: Tan 3/0 (or the body's color).
Rib: Fine gold wire.
Body: Hare's mask. (Or synthetic dubbing in any of the caddis colors described on page 49.)
Hackle: One, brown (or a color to blend with the body). The hackle is bound at the *front* of the body, spiraled back to the bend, secured with the wire rib.
Wing: Elk hair (originally, bleached). Cut the butts of the hair short and blunt and leave them as a head.
RETRIEVES: Slow, or lively and skimming.

MIKULAK SEDGE

Art Mikulak (tied by Skip)

Hook: Light wire, 2X long, sizes 12 to 6.
Thread: Eight-ought or 6/0, of the body's color.
Tail: A small bunch of stacked natural-light elk hair. (The tail is actually part of the wing.)
Body and Wing: Dubbing—dark-green (for the travelling sedge), olive, and the range from light- to chocolate-brown. The wing is two or three stacked bunches of natural-light elk hair. Dub some body, add hair, dub some more, add some hair...
Hackle: One, brown.
Head: The cut butts of the last bunch of wing-hair.
RETRIEVES: #9 (page 58).

DAMSELFLY-NYMPH IMITATIONS

OLIVE DAMSEL

Dave Whitlock (tied by Brian)

Hook: Light to heavy wire, 2X long, sizes 12 to 8.
Thread: Green 8/0 or 6/0.
Tail: Green marabou tips.
Rib: Fine gold wire.
Abdomen: Olive bright synthetic dubbing.
Wing Case and Top of Head: Green raffia.
Thorax: The same dubbing used in the abdomen.
Legs: Dyed-olive grouse or hen flank. (Brian used bunches here, but Dave lays the feather flat over the thorax.)
Eyes: Black preformed barbell eyes.
RETRIEVES: #10 and #11 (page 58).

SKIP'S FLUFFY DAMSEL

Skip Morris (tied by Skip)

Hook: Heavy wire, 1X short to standard length, sizes 12 to 8.
Thread: Dark-green 8/0 or 6/0.
Abdomen and Tail: The tip-half of a light-green, medium-green, or olive-brown marabou plume, trimmed to slender (after it's bound onto the bend).
Rib: A twisted loop of the working thread.
Thorax, Head, and Wing Case: Marabou fibers (abdomen's color), bound at the hook's bend, wrapped up the shank, secured, and ribbed.
Eyes: A length of green (brown is an alternate) Antron yarn crossways, short.
Legs: A section of split Super Floss or Flexi Floss bound behind the eyes on each side.
RETRIEVES: #10 and #11 (page 58).

DRAGONFLY-NYMPH IMITATIONS

MORRISFOAM PREDATOR

Skip Morris (tied by Skip)

Hook: Heavy wire, 2X or 3X long, sizes 12 to 6.
Thread: Brown 3/0.
Tail: (Optional) pheasant-tail fibers, short.
Back: A strip of brown or olive-brown closed-cell foam-sheeting, about 3/32-inch thick and about gape-wide.
Abdomen: Tan or pale-green rabbit, dubbed.
Head and Wing Case: A slim strip of the same foam used for the back, folded back over the eyes, trimmed and then thinned with a razor blade.
Legs: A brown rubber-strand bound at each side of the front of the abdomen.
Eyes: Preformed black plastic barbell eyes.
RETRIEVES: #12 and #13 (page 58) (or troll), but use a type-III full-sinking line.
COMMENTS: The buoyant Morrisfoam Predator swims just above the bottom, above snags (usually).

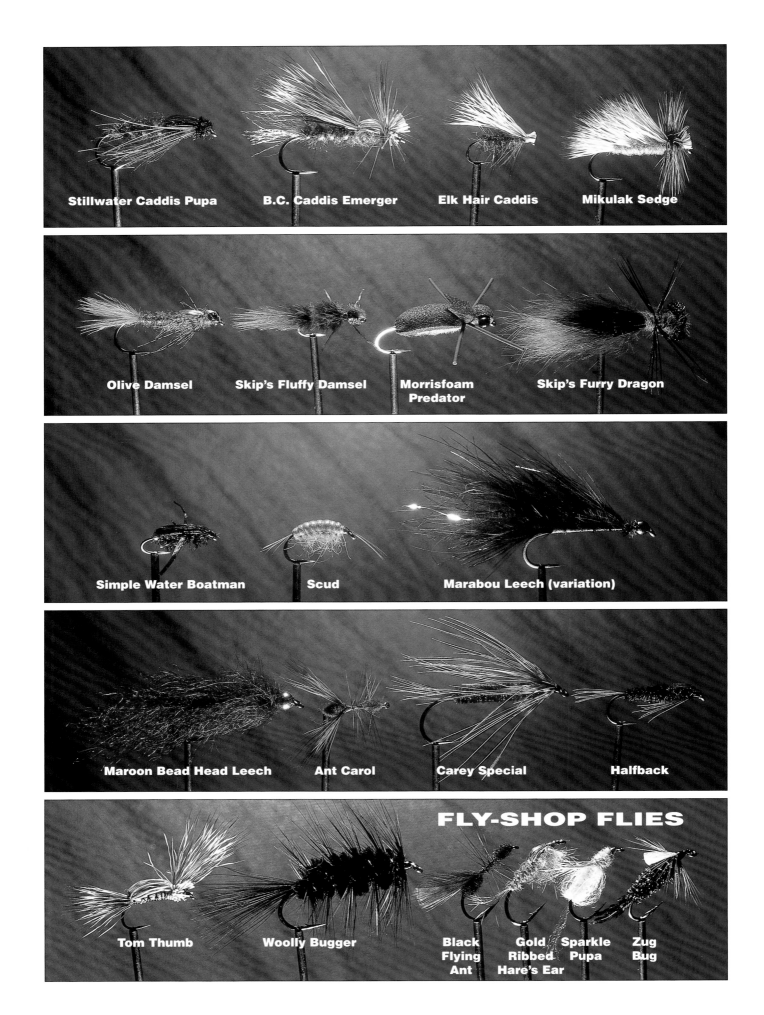

Stillwater Caddis Pupa   B.C. Caddis Emerger   Elk Hair Caddis   Mikulak Sedge

Olive Damsel   Skip's Fluffy Damsel   Morrisfoam Predator   Skip's Furry Dragon

Simple Water Boatman   Scud   Marabou Leech (variation)

Maroon Bead Head Leech   Ant Carol   Carey Special   Halfback

FLY-SHOP FLIES

Tom Thumb   Woolly Bugger   Black Flying Ant   Gold Ribbed Hare's Ear   Sparkle Pupa   Zug Bug

SKIP'S FURRY DRAGON

Skip Morris (tied by Skip)

Hook: Heavy wire, 1X short to standard length, sizes 10 to 6.
Thread: Green 8/0, 6/0 or 3/0.
Abdomen: Rabbit fur, mainly dark-green with a little brown and black, in bunches up the shank. (Or just dark-olive rabbit topped with a tiny bit of black.)
Eyes: Black or dark-gray wool yarn or a slim strip of Furry Foam (same colors) bound crossways, short.
Wing Case and Legs: Pheasant tail fibers, tips for legs, butts for wing case. (Or just a big dark-olive or brown pliant hackle, wound.)
Head and Abdomen: Dark-green rabbit, dubbed.
RETRIEVES: #12 and #13 (page 58).
COMMENTS: The Janssen Dragon, Hal Janssen's excellent fly, inspired the Skip's Furry Dragon.

WATER BOATMAN AND BACK SWIMMER IMITATION

SIMPLE WATER BOATMAN

Brian Chan (tied by Brian)

Hook: Heavy wire, 1X long, sizes 12 and 10.
Thread: Black 6/0 or 8/0.
Back: Pheasant-tail fibers, about two dozen. (I add a strip of plastic sheeting over the top.)
Body: Dark- or emerald-green plastic chenille.
Legs: Black Super Floss or Flexi Floss, threaded through the body with a needle, held with glue.
RETRIEVES: #14 (page 58).

SCUD IMITATIONS

SCUD

Al Troth (tied by Skip)

Hook: Heavy wire, 1X long, sizes 16 to 10.
Weight: One layer of lead or lead-substitute wire.
Thread: Dark-green (or just dark) 8/0 or 6/0.
Tail and Antennae: Hackle fibers of the body's color. (Many tiers omit the tail and antennae.)
Back: Clear-plastic sheeting, as in a sandwich bag.
Rib: Fine monofilament (light tippet is good).
Body: Olive-green or gray rabbit fur, dubbed.
RETRIEVES: #15 and #16 (page 58).

LEECH IMITATIONS

MARABOU LEECH (VARIATION)

Hal Janssen (tied by Skip)

Hook: Heavy wire, 2X or 3X long, sizes 10 to 4.
Thread: Three-ought of the wing's color.
Bead: Black metal, 1/8-inch diameter.
Tail: Long marabou side-fibers (wing's color), mixed with sparse Flashabou Dubbing or Lite Brite in sliver and the marabou's color (or purple with black marabou).
Wing-Body: Four or five bunches of black, brown, tan, or magenta marabou side-fibers and Flashabou Dubbing or Lite Brite in silver and the marabou's color.
Head: Marabou fiber-butts twisted with the thread.
RETRIEVES: #17 and #18 (page 58).
COMMENTS: A slightly flashy, very active imitation based on Hal's original.

MAROON BEAD HEAD LEECH

Brian Chan (tied by Brian)

Hook: Heavy wire, 2X or 3X long, sizes 8 and 6.
Thread: Black 8/0 or 6/0.
Bead: Gold (brass), 1/8-inch diameter.
Tail and Body: Black/red Arizona Simi-Seal or Black n' Red Dazzle dubbing, a long tuft for a tail, in a dubbing loop for the body.
RETRIEVES: #17 and #18 (page 58).

TERRESTRIAL IMITATIONS

ANT CAROL

Skip Morris (tied by Skip)

Hook: Light wire, standard length or 1X long (standard dry-fly hook), sizes 16 to 8.
Thread: Eight-ought or 6/0 of the abdomen's color.
Abdomen: Orange-red (or black or brown) synthetic dubbing, built up to round or slightly elongated.
Wings: Brown buck tail, stacked, angling back.
Hackle: One, of the abdomen's color, in a few spiraled turns over bare thread in the hook's center.
Thorax: The abdomen's dubbing built up to a ball.
RETRIEVES: Cast it to ant-seeking trout and then leave it still or twitch it barely.
COMMENTS: The name of this fly comes from what my niece and nephew call my wife. In varied colors and sizes it can imitate all sorts of flying ants.

ALL-PURPOSE FLIES

CAREY SPECIAL

Colonel Carey and Dr. Lloyd Day
(tied by Skip)

Hook: Heavy wire, 2X to 4X long, sizes 10 to 4.
Thread: Black 8/0, 6/0, or 3/0.
Tail: Pheasant-rump fibers.
Body: Peacock herl. (All kinds of body materials are used for Careys; my favorite alternate is thick dark-green or dark-olive chenille.)
Hackle: One pheasant-rump feather.
RETRIEVES: Depends on what it's imitating, which most often is dragon nymphs, but can be almost any big insect. Careys are very popular trolling flies, too.

HALFBACK

John Dexheimer (tied by Brian)

Hook: Heavy wire, 2X or 3X long, sizes 12 to 8.
Thread: Black 8/0 or 6/0.
Tail: Brown hackle fibers or pheasant-tail fibers.
Abdomen and Thorax: Peacock herl.
Wing Case: Pheasant-tail fibers.
Legs: The tips of the wing-case fibers tucked under and bound, or hackle fibers as a beard.
RETRIEVES: Depends on what it's imitating—damsel nymphs, mayfly nymphs, caddis larvae, whatever. The Halfback is also a good trolling fly.

TOM THUMB

(tied by Brian)

Hook: Light wire, standard length to 1X long (standard dry-fly hook), sizes 16 to 8. (Some fine lake fishers prefer to tie this fly short on a long-shank hook, claiming that it hooks far more trout tied this way.)
Thread: Black or gray 8/0 or 6/0, but I prefer heavier thread, 3/0 or even flat waxed nylon.
Tail: Deer hair, stacked.
Hump and Wing: Deer hair, stacked, one bunch for all, pulled forward and bound. The hairs tips form a fanlike wing, as on the Sparkle Dun (whose pattern is listed in this chapter).
RETRIEVES: Depends upon what you want it to imitate—caddis adults, buzzing back swimmers, whatever.
COMMENTS: There seem to be as many ways to tie a Tom Thumb as there are tiers who tie it. Brian ties it as here, with a modest tail and a head of deer-hair butts. But long tails are common; as are long wings. However it's tied, it's always a great skimming fly. And excellent for top-water trolling.

WOOLLY BUGGER

Russell Blessing (tied by Skip)

Hook: Heavy wire, 3X long, sizes 14 to 2.
Thread: Eight-ought, 6/0, or 3/0 of the body's color.
Tail: One marabou plume (of the body's color), shank to full-hook length.
Hackle: One, of the body's color, spiraled up the body as five to eight ribs.
Body: Black, magenta, olive, or brown chenille.
RETRIEVES: Depends on what it's imitating, which is usually a leech or a dragon nymph.
COMMENTS: Some tiers wind the hackle *back,* then wind fine copper wire *forward* through the hackle to reinforce it (as in the sample fly). This fly can roughly imitate much. And it's very popular with trollers.

FLY-SHOP FLIES

Though Brian and I seldom fish the four flies listed below (preferring the previous 36), they are all fine flies with fine records to prove their worthiness. So we show them here not for the tier but as samples for the non-tying angler to help him find them for purchasing. All are included on our "Introductory Selection of Flies" on page 60, earlier in this chapter. (all tied by Skip)

BLACK FLYING ANT

GOLD RIBBED HARE'S EAR

SPARKLE PUPA

(Green and brown are most common, but there are many possible colors.)

ZUG BUG

9

The broad subject of fly casting, from its basics to its fine points with regards to fishing lakes, is far too much ground to cover here. So learn from this chapter what lakes will require of your casting; then, if you need to, find a good casting book or casting instructor, learn, and *practice*.

Important point: don't wait to practice your casting until you are on a lake. Practice, if you need it (as most of us do), is best without the distraction of fish and fishing, when full concentration can be given the rod, arm, and line.

With no current to negotiate, you won't need all those clever stream-casts that throw strategic waves in fly line—in lakes, the simple straight-line cast is always right.

DISTANCE

The long cast—50, 60, even 80 feet, the kind you've probably been told to avoid on streams—is the standard cast on lakes. Lake-fishing situations that demand long casts are many; here are just a few: keeping a nymph down working along a shoal just as long as possible for the best

odds of trout meeting fly, keeping a fly down for any real time at all in water so deep that most of the line is used up just in reaching depth, and pushing the fly far out to cover that distant rise. A narrow line-loop and high line-speed are the elements that make casts long. Such line-loops and line-speeds result from efficient technique (and practice, of course). Efficient long casts require only a modest use of force, and excessive force can never be efficiency's substitute.

Many good lake fishers find long casts less tiring if they add to them a single or double "haul," a quick, short tug on the line at the rod-tip's final fastest point in the stroke.

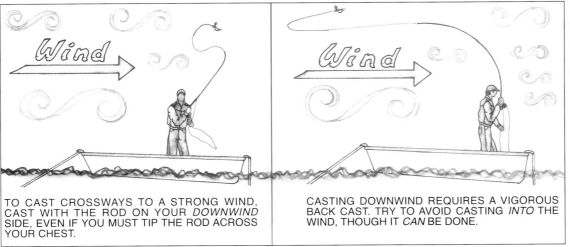

TO CAST CROSSWAYS TO A STRONG WIND, CAST WITH THE ROD ON YOUR *DOWNWIND* SIDE, EVEN IF YOU MUST TIP THE ROD ACROSS YOUR CHEST.

CASTING DOWNWIND REQUIRES A VIGOROUS BACK CAST. TRY TO AVOID CASTING *INTO* THE WIND, THOUGH IT *CAN* BE DONE.

CASTING STRATEGIES FOR WIND

WIND

The only dependably windless fishing I know of is in tiny streams lying deep within draws and cocooned in thick timber. I hear a lot about wind on lakes, and though it's true that they are usually exposed to its full force, some of the mightiest winds I've wrestled with swept through river can-

yons or river valleys. Wind is a familiar challenge in nearly all fly fishing. And coping with wind is as much strategy as skill.

If the wind is just too strong to fish in, perhaps it is also too strong to be fishing in safely.

MORRIS & CHAN ON FLY FISHING TROUT LAKES

SINKING LINE

The floating line is so nearly always appropriate for trout streams that it's the only line most fly fishers ever bring to them. Lakes are another matter altogether—for them the floating line, though common enough, is the exception, while the sinking line is the standard. As a result, stream fishers (or anyone who's fished only floating lines) often have some adjustments to make in order to comfortably cast the sinking lines of lakes. But casting sinking lines is not so much harder than casting floating lines; it's mostly just *different*.

The first important difference is, the caster can lift a considerable length of floating line from the water whereas he can lift only a few feet of sinking line. Which is just as well, because trout often take a sunken fly little more than a leader's length from a boat.

The second important difference is, a floating line's lightweight bulk casts almost as though it hovers, while a finer, denser sinking line feels always as though it's dropping. To compensate for this relative dropping, the caster must *slightly* quicken his strokes and *slightly* shorten his pauses between them.

PICKING UP A FLOATING LINE TO CAST

PICKING UP
LINE TO CAST

LINE
(a few feet only)

LEADER

PICKING UP A SINKING LINE

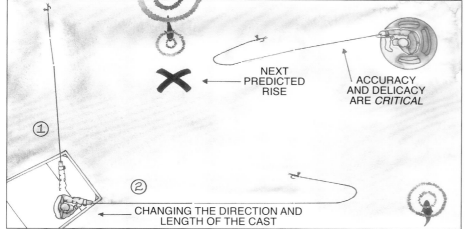

NEXT
PREDICTED
RISE

ACCURACY
AND DELICACY
ARE *CRITICAL*

① ②

CHANGING THE DIRECTION AND
LENGTH OF THE CAST

CHANGING DIRECTION IN CASTING

RISING AND SHALLOW TROUT

To effectively fish in lakes for surface-feeding trout, one must cast accurately and be able to delicately drop a fly near a trout's rise. Surface-feeding trout also demand that you can quickly change the direction or length of your cast, and sometimes both.

Skittish trout in shallow water make pretty much these same demands of the caster's versatility and skill.

AVOIDING TROUBLE

You make an efficient stroke sending the line out in a narrow, almost poetic arc. At precisely the correct moment you release the line to watch it rush out the guides, and it does, for a split second...then—thud!—the line jars to a stop. It drops to the water in chaotic squiggles. Your foot was on the line you meant to shoot. You consequently blew your cast. (But it was so elegant up until then...wasn't it?)

Shooting line is part of making long casts (and long casts are part of lake fishing), but it only works if the line to be shot is clear. In a float tube or other inflatable you can spoil line-shooting by letting the line drop outside the stripping apron or getting something into the apron that can catch the line.

In a boat, the problem is usually a foot standing on the line, but it can also be a tackle-box, oarlocks, or such. The solution for boats is to follow this sequence: (1.) gather the line in coils on the floor of the boat as you retrieve the fly (2.) check to see that the coiled line is clear of snags and feet, and then clear it if necessary (3.) promise yourself this: I will *not* move my feet, and then (4.) make the cast and shoot the line.

10 BOATS, FLOAT TUBES, AND TACKLE

Before we begin, understand that you do not need *all* the stuff that follows. You do, however, need some of it. I'll make clear what is required and what is optional at the end of this chapter.

WATERCRAFT AND THEIR ACCESSORIES

"Watercraft"—such a bland word. But what other heading could contain everything from ostentatious inner tubes to speedboats? Having fished in watercraft from every category to come, I speak on the subject with the pleasant (though unfamiliar) feeling of authority that comes from full-range experience. Brian's experience is strongly at work here too, of course, as always. What follows are your choices in watercraft and, from Brian's and my perspectives, considerations to help you choose wisely. But don't be surprised if you choose more than one because each type of watercraft can do things the others cannot, thus few serious lake fishers own but one.

THE FLOAT TUBE AND ITS RELATIVES

THE ESSENTIAL FLOAT TUBE

The float tube consists of a seat in a fabric sheath containing a large "O"-shaped bladder. The standard trappings include a "stripping apron," to hold loose line; a backrest of fabric over a small bladder; and pockets for tackle, food, drink, whatever.

Advantages: The biggest advantage of the float tube is its low cost. Other advantages include its small bulk, so easy to transport and launch; the freedom of both hands for casting and fishing; the angler's half-submerged position, offering so little for the wind to play with; excellent control of speed and direction when trolling; and exercise from the constant working of swim fins.

Disadvantages: The float tube is deathly slow—even a rowboat is much quicker. Carrying space in a float tube, like speed, is restricted, though no more than when wading and fishing a stream. Entering and exiting the tube can be awkward. The angler's low position in the water restricts his field of view. And sitting down in waders and water hour after hour, though sometimes pleasant, is sometimes not.

U-BOAT

Following the float tube's alphabet theme of a letter-"O" shape, the U-boat is shaped like the letter "U." The result is a sort of open-ended float tube. (The German U-boat submarine is no relation to the U-boat float tube and the latter, if well-constructed, should neither resemble nor perform as does the former.) Many U-boats have a bar that locks across their opening after the angler is in; then a crotch-strap is buckled to the bar. But some U-boats have no bar or strap—the angler simply sits down and fin-flips away.

Advantages and Disadvantages: Really just a variation of the float tube, the U-boat's only significant difference with its progenitor is that entering and exiting it is much easier (which can matter).

KICK-BOAT

The kick-boat is shaped like the letter "Z"... No, I'm lying. Borrowing from both the float tube and the boat, the kick-boat in its various forms can lean towards either. While most kick-boats are propelled by fins, like the float tube, an increasing number rely on oars, like the rowboat—many take both oars *and* fins, but some such hybrids are poor with fins and good with oars, or the reverse. A warning: if the boat doesn't hold you completely above the water, rowing may be inefficient as a result of drag.

Advantages and Disadvantages: More expensive than most float tubes or U-boats, sometimes less expensive than true boats, kick-boats usually offer much more carrying space than float tubes and

U-boats, the trade-off being more bulk and weight (though both are usually still well under that of a true boat). Speed? A good rowing kick-boat is a match for a rowboat, but fins are always slow. Kick-boats vary so much in design that it's hard to evaluate them as a whole—bear this in mind when shopping for one.

WADERS, BOOTS, AND FINS

Waders are a requirement for all float tubes and U-boats, and most kick-boats. The exception to this rule is my friend Arnie, who boldly wears only hip boots while perched on the high seat of his kick-boat—and whom I suspect of frequently concealing a wet posterior (as we all should).

Neoprene waders are the warmest, and therefore the safest choice since trout-water is seldom less than chilly. Waders of lighter materials will require plenty of insulating clothing beneath. Several of my friends are fans of the "breathable" waders. Water stays out, air circulates, so that the standard soaking of perspiration is dodged—that's the theory. So far, in our brief experience with breathables, Brian and I have found ours dry, comfortable, and cool—too cool in lakes except in summer.

Many anglers wear neoprene boots ("booties") over the feet of their stocking-foot (bootless) waders and under their fins. These boots give the fins something to grip while protecting the waders when the wearer waddles about on shore (walking in fins is always waddling).

Swim fins are the standard propellant for float tubes, U-boats, and kick-boats. There are many variations of style, and seasoned anglers' opinions as to which style is best are equally varied, so the best advice is, look around and ask around. Prices of fins vary as greatly as styles and opinions on styles.

BOATS

The range of size in fly-fishing boats is broad, from small as tiny kick-boats to near live-aboard size complete with the thrust to skim several anglers swiftly along. Of course most boats are larger than this smallest example and smaller than this largest. Boat design varies just as much as boat size. Each size and each design has fly fishers who are devoted to it. Here is a brief rundown:

INFLATABLE BOAT

If you already own a good inflatable, use it—it will probably make a serviceable lake-boat—but there are better choices.

Advantages: Some top-drawer inflatables are sturdy, row well, have solid flooring (for comfortable standing), comfortable seats, and a transom that will take an outboard motor. Some inflatable boats pack down modestly small.

Disadvantages: Inexpensive toylike inflatables often leak and seldom support a real sitting position, leaving the angler half-prone and soaked. They also are seldom seaworthy, so bring the life vests and go with caution. Good inflatable boats can easily be as

expensive as wood and aluminum boats. Their swollen sides take up useful room and if those sides are high-quality, their thick skin will make the inflatable as heavy as many comparable fiberglass and aluminum boats. If the inflation valves are exposed, they can constantly tangle with fly lines. Finally, when changing elevations you'll have to adjust inflation—unmonitored inflatables can overswell and strain or rupture in thinning air.

CANOE

Though pleasant transportation, a canoe is at best just adequate for fly fishing in lakes. A canoe turns slowly and demands a lot of attention at the paddle. It is also unstable and therefore demands concentration to keep it upright. While it is certainly possible to fly fish from a canoe, and there are fly fishers who prefer to (usually, I suspect, out of sentimentalism), there are better craft for the job. We've all seen canoes, so no photo here.

Advantages: None, unless you already own one. **Disadvantages:** Too many to suit most fly fishers.

ROWBOAT

Wood, aluminum, and fiberglass all make a fine rowboat, though wood is the most elegant, heaviest, and requires the most upkeep of the three. There are many standard designs for rowboats—pram, johnboat, dory, punt, to name but a few. Brian's favorite boat for lakes is the low, broad johnboat. (Though he also likes small prams.) A keel-less curved-hull drift-boat for rivers can be serviceable on lakes. In any case, a rowboat for lakes must row well and be fairly wide and fairly flat-hulled, for stable, comfortable standing.

Under nine-feet is comfortable only for one angler.

Advantages: Rowboats row swiftly, quietly, and efficiently, and are much faster than float-tubes and fins. This makes the rowboat my first choice for chasing rising trout (though some rowing kick-boats can compete). There is space to stand, sit, and stretch and for storage.

Disadvantages: Somewhat costly; somewhat large and bulky (when compared, for example, with a float tube); larger models are difficult for one person to handle on shore; and when anchors are in, oars engage hands that could be managing rod and line.

POWER BOAT

I think of a power boat as a boat too large to easily row—the definition I'll use here. (Though a small rowboat with a small outboard motor is technically a power boat, and does take on many power-boat qualities.)

A too-large-to-easily-row boat, I'd say, is 12 feet long to as long as 16. With a gasoline or high-thrust electric outboard motor (inboard motors are rare in lake boats) such a boat can move quickly around a large lake. Some serious lake fishers use a big gasoline outboard to get from place to place, and a small electric outboard for maneuvering.

The standard design for lake-boats over 9 feet long is the "johnboat," low, wide, and flat. In the largest lake-boats, conventional peaked-bottom hull designs become practical.

Advantages: The chief advantage of a power boat is speed. Catching one hatch across the lake, then a different one back near the boat-launch, covering a series of scattered springs or creek mouths— it's surprising once you have that speed how often you use it. Room for fishing and storage is plentiful, of course. Power boats are best with large lakes, at least a half-mile across.

Disadvantages: Size and its outboard motor comprise a power boat's main disadvantages. Only the smallest power boats can be carried and launched without a boat-trailer and its attendant cost and storage and waiting your turn at the boat-launch on busy days. The outboard motor requires maintenance and fussing and fuel or a battery. On little lakes, a power boat may be too much, almost clumsy, and on some lakes gasoline outboards are banned, an opportunity to discover the ease—or strain—with which your boat rows.

LIFE VEST

From state to state, marine-safety laws vary, and there are federal (Coast Guard) laws you must also obey. I always wear a vest when I'm in a moving power boat. And the idea of a life vest in a float tube now seems more reasonable to me than it once did. Check with your sheriff's department concerning state law regarding vests, the Coast Guard for federal law, and bear in mind that you can only be safer wearing a life vest or with one near at hand.

ANCHOR

Float tubes and such are small enough to require only a single lightweight anchor, and there are several designed just for that purpose.

Any boat will demand two substantial anchors. There are many designs; each has its believers.

After twenty years of fiddling with boats and anchors, Brian suggests the following:

For boats of 12 feet and shorter: two anchors, at least 8-pounds each.

For boats of 14 to 16 feet: two anchors, at least 10 pounds each (Brian prefers 12 pounds).

BOATS, FLOAT TUBES, AND TACKLE

FLY ROD

During the decade in which I designed and constructed graphite and fiberglass fly rods for my living (yes, *designed*—the rod-shaft-manufacturing plants followed precisely my diagrams and specifications), I developed some opinions. However, you shouldn't take my opinions, or anyone else's, too seriously. Selecting a fly rod is a very personal matter. What matters most is that a rod satisfies you, pleases you—feels right. (And, of course, that it's up to the job.)

Trout-lake fishing often requires long casts, the kind that everyone warns you are to be avoided on streams. Such casts require a rod long enough for good leverage, but not so long as to be too tiring. Brian likes 9- to 9 1/2-foot rods for lakes; I like 8 1/2 to 9. The angler deep in a float tube or low-seat kick-boat might prefer a longish rod to help keep back-casts airborne. But don't expect a long rod to work wonders—even a 12-footer won't hoist a dropped back-cast. Practice, not longer rods, is usually the solution to casting problems.

A trout-lake rod should lean towards powerful, but only a modest lean—a rod with a quick and lively spring, but not unyielding stiffness. I suggest that that rod have a fairly stout bottom-half to help make long, quick casts.

Lake fishers often keep two or more rods rigged for quick switching. Expect to collect a few rods over time.

Materials? Forget split-bamboo unless you already have it—some wonderful rods are made from it, but they cost dearly, take little abuse, and are really for aficionados. Fiberglass is tough and reasonably priced. There are some fine glass rods, but much over 8 feet long they get a bit heavy. But a good glass 8-footer is a solid lake rod. Graphite, of course, is the standard these days for all fly fishing, and especially apt for the typically long casts of lakes. It is very light and fairly tough. Expensive? Not necessarily.

FLY LINE

To the lake fisher, fly lines are even more important than reels, and perhaps as important as rods.

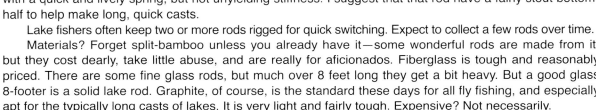

Weight: This describes the actual weight of the first 30 feet of line. I use mostly 5-weight lines for trout lakes, as does Brian. The 6-weight has the advantage in the wind, but 5 is nearly always heavy enough and beats the 6 for finesse with rising trout. Bottom line: for a serious all-around sequence of lake-fishing lines don't go lighter than 5 or heavier than 7.

Taper: Most common are the double taper (constant diameter except at the ends) and weight forward (most of its weight in its first 30 feet, followed by thin running-line). In a floating line, you can go with either. But Brian and I agree that weight-forward tapers are best for all sinking lines.

The two standard fly-line tapers.

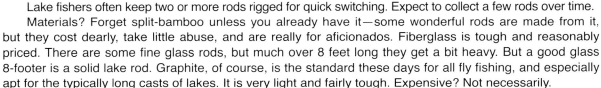

Floating and Sinking Lines: The serious lake fisher finds use for and eventually owns several fly lines of varying densities: a full-floating, a type I (also called an "intermediate" line, though there remains some mystery as to whether the two lines are one or are slightly different; it sinks very slowly), a type II (sinks modestly), a type III (sinks quickly), and sometimes even a type IV (hell-bent on finding the lake bed). But you can begin with as few as two lines (see "Essentials Only" at the end of this chapter).

There are "sink-tip" lines (the tip sinks, the rest floats) and "full-sinking" lines (*everything* sinks). Brian and I use only the latter for lakes—it's too much work getting a sink-tip down and keeping it there.

For floating lines, Brian and I prefer pale colors (which blend into

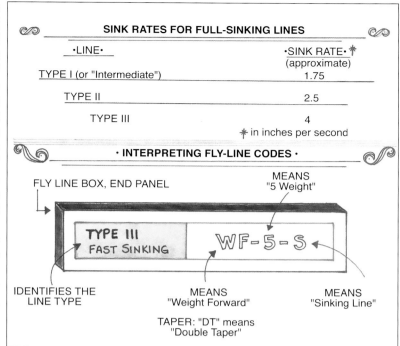

SINK RATES FOR FULL-SINKING LINES	
·LINE·	·SINK RATE·✳ (approximate)
TYPE I (or "Intermediate")	1.75
TYPE II	2.5
TYPE III	4

✳ in inches per second

· INTERPRETING FLY-LINE CODES ·

FLY LINE BOX, END PANEL

MEANS "5 Weight"

TYPE III FAST SINKING

WF-5-S

IDENTIFIES THE LINE TYPE

MEANS "Weight Forward"

MEANS "Sinking Line"

TAPER: "DT" means "Double Taper"

pale sky from the trout's view) and dark colors for sinking (which blend into dark lake-bed).

Odd but useful is the "stillwater" line from Scientific Anglers. It's clear, like leader; sinks at a rate between type I and II; and is a blessing with cautious trout in air-clear water. And sometimes its odd sink-rate can be just right.

Behind a fly line is backing, to handle the long runs of big trout. Brian (who knows better than I) recommends at least 50 yards of 20-pound Dacron. He *prefers* 100 yards.

REEL

Like fly reels for most fishing, a reel for lake fishing is a simple affair—just a frame, drag, handle, and spool. It must have space for the line and an ample amount of backing, it must operate smoothly—never seize or stall—and changing its spools must be reasonably easy. All this can be found in a good reel of modest price.

Here are the essentials of fly reels in general from the lake fisher's slant in particular: The straightforward "single-action" reel, with handle mounted directly to spool, remains the standard. Most fly reels feature an adjustable "drag," which makes smooth resistance (at least, it *should* be smooth) against the whirling spool. This controls the spool's momentum to avoid a fly-line tangle. Much of the cost of a reel lies in the smoothness and dependability of its drag. Spool capacity (and therefore, reel capacity) is normally no measure of quality, only of size. But do choose a large enough reel to contain the fly line and plenty of backing (read about backing in the previous caption). The serious lake fisher uses so many different lines that he finds himself collecting extra spools for each of his reels. Expect to eventually own some extra spools.

LEADER

Though I'm sure one could make do on lakes with a single length and weight of leader for all lines and uses, there are good reasons for using a modest assortment.

Despite knotted, braided-butt, fluoro-carbon, and other leaders, each with its attendant theory as to why it's superior for this or that or just every-thing altogether, the standard for lakes is the simple knotless tapered kind. It remains an excellent choice and the only one we'll investigate further. But play with the others if you like—many of the theories behind them seem perfectly plausible.

The butt of a leader may be knotted directly to the fly line or knot-ted to a short length of stout, level monofilament that remains with the line through the lives of several lead-ers. If you choose the latter, consider this short stout extension part of the leader's total length.

Tippet: At the point of a pre-tapered leader the angler adds a few feet of "tippet," fine monofilament of constant diameter. Leader and tippet come separate, and the angler knots them together. The tippet should be one size lighter than the leader, so a leader whose tip is 4X would commonly take a tippet of 5X. This "X" business is odd and confusing, but basically, the higher the number preceding the "X," the finer the material. You could simply go by a tippet's breaking strength, but the "X" is traditional and well-established.

Here are Brian's and my general recommendations for leader lengths and strengths.

- For sinking lines, deep: 9 feet long with a point of 3X knotted to two feet of 4X tippet.
- For floating line-deep fly:12 feet long with a point of 4X knotted to four feet of 5X tippet.
- For floating-line fishing to surface-feeding trout: 9 feet with a point of 4X knotted to three feet of 5X tippet.

These guidelines are, of course, only a starting point. Conditions and fish-size are always important—what good is 5X tippet with a seven-pound rainbow back in the reeds? And with brilliant sunshine lighting every detail in clear water, will big trout overlook the 2X tippet it takes to restrain them from the peril of sunken trees? When there is no good solution, the thrill of hooking and losing trout must be enough.

And sometimes it is.

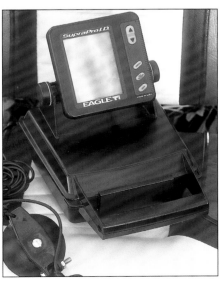

FISH FINDER

This is the standard argument against the fish finder: It is (if you'll excuse the trendy cliche') "hi-tech." This is my argument against that argument: Polarized sun glasses do the same work on streams, do it better, and are also high-tech, so if you use the one, you are a hypocrite to criticize the other. And polarized sun glasses border the nostrils of nearly all these critics.

Algae bloom, air bubbles, tree limbs, plankton, and other deceivers can show on a finder as fish—the finder's instructions help the user judge the readings. What I like my finder for most is reading a lake's bed. The screen shows me level mud or silt (with its promise of chironomids, Libellulidae dragons, *Hexagenia* may-flies, and other dwellers of the ooze); it shows me plants (where scuds, damselflies, and other vegetation-lovers may thrive), wood debris, drop-offs—you get the idea.

Brian prefers a finder whose sonar cone spreads 40 to 90 degrees. Smaller cones, he feels, tell too little.

VEST OR BOX

The fisherman's vest is a sound solution for the angler who needs to carry leaders, boxes of flies, and more in an unobstructed way as he wades. But seldom is there a need to wade in trout lakes. Many fly fishers stay with the vest even in a boat, just because a vest seems somehow wedded with a fly rod. As a practical matter, though, a vest in a boat winds up bunched on a seat (from which it usually dangles and drops) becoming a puzzle when the angler searches the heap for pockets and items. The float-tube angler who brings a vest must wear it, in which case it does its work well. But why wear bulk and weight that could instead be neatly stored in the tube's built-in pockets?

I carry a trout-lake tackle box. (It is actually a tool box, much better, I feel, than the real tackle boxes I inspected with their multitude of tiny trays for which I found so little use.) I also carry a hip-box that slings from the shoulder and straps round the waist for wading, yet also straps securely to my Breezerider U-boat for fishing lakes. Be it tackle box, hip-box, or chest pack, something that stands up and holds its shape and contains a few compartments or pockets is a blessing for fishing from boats.

HOOK REMOVER

"Forceps," long slender pliers with loops for thumb and finger, are the established tool for removing flies from trout. There are now, however, some other ingenious tools for this work, and they, too, do the job.

Few experienced fly fishers would intentionally go fishing without a hook remover.

CLIPPERS AND HOOK HONE

The fly fishers with notched front teeth are the ones who don't bother with clippers. Things go better if you do use clippers—fly fishers, after all, are so often tying and trimming knots. Everyday fingernail clippers are good, as are clippers especially made for fly fishers. Whichever you choose, attach them to your vest or carry them in your tackle box.

Hook hones range from fine-tooth files to tiny sharpening stones. All seem to do the job, which is to sharpen a fly-hook's point. Most modern fly-hooks need no sharpening when new, but they will often need it before the fly is lost or worn out. A good test is to let a fly hang with its point on your thumbnail, then try to draw the fly *lightly* across the nail. If the fly catches or scratches the nail, it's sharp; if it slides freely off, sharpen.

NET

So far as Brian and I are concerned, a net is indispensible in fishing lakes. A net with soft mesh, such as cotton or nylon, can check a trout gently and quickly, so that the angler can unhook and release the trout without doing it harm. Brian prefers that the squares of the mesh not exceed 1/2 inch across.

STRINGER

If you plan to kill a trout (which Brian and I, like most fly fishers, seldom do) crack it hard a few times between the eyes with something hard and heavy (see "Priest" below); then store it dry and cool and gut it soon. Dragging a trout around on a stringer is cruel—shove a wire up your nose and out your mouth and then have a friend drag *you* around by it; then you'll understand.

PRIEST

A fisherman's priest is what a thug would call a "blackjack," a little club for braining someone or something (in this case, a trout). I don't carry one; I simply find a stick for this work on those rare occasions when I kill a trout. Occasionally a trout is mortally injured by the hook, and then the priest (or a substitute) should deliver the last rites.

THERMOMETER

Don't let this intimidate you—you needn't have a degree in entomology or fisheries biology to benefit from knowing water temperature. Until I got a fish finder, my heavy metal-shielded thermometer on a long cord also helped me gauge depth. (See "Weather," in Chapter 6, on page 40, for more on using a thermometer.)

WEIGHT, FLOATANT, AND STRIKE INDICATOR

Tiny split shot or lead putty can be added to a leader to draw an imitation chironomid pupa on a floating line down deep. The lead is attached up from the fly a couple of feet. There are now substitutes for lead, born of the belief that lead is harmful to waterfowl. (And if it's bad for waterfowl, isn't it likely bad for other lake inhabitants?)

Dry flies nearly always require a light massaging of fly floatant in order to stay afloat for long (same for leaders). The standard floatant is paste, but some are a liquid in which the fly is briefly bathed.

A strike indicator has but one purpose in fishing lakes: to buoy a sunken fly on a floating line. Usually that fly is an imitation chironomid pupa, but it can be other things, such as an imitation chironomid *larva*, mayfly nymph, damselfly nymph—whatever the trout want that tips skyward and moves slightly and slowly (which perhaps the mayfly and damselfly seldom do, but imitations work this way sometimes; who knows why?). The position of the indicator on the leader controls the fly's depth. The putty and cork indicators shown here are currently popular, but indicators can be yarn, cork, putty, foam, or practically anything buoyant.

I have used indicators so often in fishing rivers that I naturally prefer them on lakes. Brian avoids them whenever he can, going to them only if trout are feeding up in the in-between depths or because he sees that I am using one and outfishing him (outfishing Brian, a rare occasion). When he does use one it is with grim expression and eyes narrowed as though facing a strong wind, even when the day is calm.

GLASSES

Polarized sunglasses cut through surface glare, carrying the angler's gaze down to the inner workings of a trout lake—it's really quite remarkable how much they'll let you see in a clear lake under bright sunshine. But the fly fisher's most important use of any kind of glasses is to protect the eyes—casts gone wrong can mean fly-hooks randomly whipping around the angler's head. For the dim hours or dark days, clear prescription glasses provide eye-protection. If your eyesight needs no correction, wear safety glasses (from a hardware store) or have an optometrist make you some clear glasses of plain flat glass in place of prescription lenses.

SUNSCREEN

Unless you fish only before sunrise, after sunset, at night, or all three, you must wear sunscreen on all exposed skin (except, perhaps, for the very tips of the fingers). You'll get more sun in a couple of hours of midday lake fishing (or most any kind of fishing)—sunny or cloudy regardless—than any sane person would submit to, considering what we now know about sun and skin cancer. There are now even lip balms that are supposedly sunscreens. Just how much skin will be exposed and in need of sunscreen brings us to the next topic.

CLOTHING

There are three reasons for wearing clothing while fishing: (1) to keep warm, (2) to protect the skin from sun exposure, and (3) to satisfy society. Bring plenty of clothing, so that you can add or reduce by layers, as a day's fishing often runs the range of cold to hot.

Wear a hat any time you are fishing in daylight. The longer and broader its bill, the more protection it will provide from sunlight. (One of my hats includes a shroud that surrounds and protects some of my face. Looks funny, but protects well.) Brian and I recommend long-sleeve shirts in all weather. Long pants, too—warm in cold air, protective in sun. I've worn heavy warm gloves while fishing every month of the year—wind, rain, and cold can come any time, often unexpectedly. Light fingerless gloves protect hands from sunlight. Brian and I always bring a rain-jacket and rain-pants when we fish lakes; they

not only shed rain but protect against chill wind and provide warmth.

Clothing for cold weather: A hat (perhaps with ear flaps), glasses, layered shirts, warm gloves (two pair), warm pants, thick socks, waterproof shoes or boots, rain-jacket and rain-pants.

Clothing for warm weather: A hat, glasses, layered light shirts, light fingerless gloves, lightweight pants, light socks, light shoes, rain-jacket and rain-pants.

THROAT PUMP

It's normally called a "stomach pump," which is part of the problem. It *should* draw up samples from the rim of a trout's *throat*—*not* from its *stomach*. Used poorly, it becomes a tool for torture and murder, which is probably why even its mention ignites debate. Use it only on trout over 12 inches long. And use it correctly or not at all.

If you plan to use a throat pump, empty it first of any water, depress its bulb, slip it gently straight into a trout's mouth until you feel the tube lightly bump the constriction at the base of the throat. Then let the bulb reinflate, and draw out the pump. Suction water into the pump, and then squirt it into a white bowl or dish. Often you'll get nothing because the trout had already swallowed. But never—*never*—force the pump in a fish.

INCIDENTALS

Water: A parched throat diminishes the joy of good fishing, and who is willing to leave good fishing for a glass of water? Bring some kind of non-alcoholic drink with you when you go out.

Food: Bring food for the same reasons as you would bring drink.

Moisturizer: Highly alkaline water is rich; insects flourish in it and trout grow fast feeding upon those insects. But such water is also extremely drying on the hands, making moisturizer more a necessity than a convenience.

Camera: Even a cheap little camera can be a blessing when a great scene is recognized or a great trout landed.

Toilet paper: I always bring a half-empty roll in a waterproof sandwich-bag. Why? I think you know why.

ESSENTIALS ONLY

The following constitutes the minimum you'll need in order to start fishing trout lakes. It is a base from which you can build. As to specific brands and models, a reputable fly shop or mail-order house can provide sound current advice. No need to spend a great deal—a collection of sound, conservative tackle is always dependable and can later be used as back-up for your final, seasoned choices or as a loaner for friends.

WATERCRAFT

A float tube or one of its inflatable relatives is a fine choice for the beginning lake fisher, portable, inexpensive, efficient. Boats can be rented at some lake-side resorts, and fly shops often rent float tubes, waders, and fins.

WADERS

You'll need them only for float tubes and U-boats, and not always for kick-boats, never for boats.

FINS

You'll need them only if you need waders (as described in the previous topic).

LIFE VEST

Bringing along one or more life vests is a matter of choice and sometimes law. (See "Life Vest" in this chapter, on page 71.)

ANCHOR

One for a float tube or its kin, two for a boat. Fishing a lake without anchoring is tough.

ROD

One rod, 8 1/2 to 9 feet in length for six-weight lines (five-weight as a second choice), moderate to slightly stiff-butt action, and overall leaning slightly towards powerful. If you want a rod strictly for lakes or an all-around light trout rod, choose a five-weight. But a six-weight rod will handle lakes and small trout streams yet perform efficiently on smallmouth and even largemouth bass. In fact, I've landed many 20-pound Pacific salmon on six-weight rods and lines. Prefer graphite but don't discount good fiberglass rods of 8 1/2 feet or shorter.

LINES

Brian and I agree: Start with one full-floating line and one type III *full-sinking* line (*no* sink-tips). The line weight should match the rod you've chosen. Beginners will want both lines in weight-forward taper. Experienced anglers may chose double-taper for floating lines, but full-sinkers are always weight-forward.

When you are ready to invest in a third line, you can take Brian's advice and get a full-sinking type I, or my advice and get a type II. By the time selecting a third line becomes an issue, you'll probably have a good sense of which will best suit your needs.

REEL

To begin with, you'll need one reel with two interchangeable spools—a spool for each of your two lines.

The reel should function smoothly and have close enough tolerances around the spool that line doesn't snag there too easily. Such a reel can be modest in cost.

LEADER

Start with six tapered leaders: two that are 9 feet long with a 3X point, two that are 9 feet long with a 4X point, and two that are 12 feet long with a 4X point.

TIPPET

Two spools of tippet: one 4X, one 5X.

VEST OR BOX

You'll need something to hold your flies, leaders, and the rest. (See "Vest or Box" earlier in this chapter, on page 75.)

HOOK REMOVER, CLIPPERS, HOOK HONE, AND NET

You'll need all these, and each is covered earlier in this chapter, on page 75.

GLASSES

Required for protecting eyes from flies. (See "Glasses" earlier in this chapter, on page 76)

CLOTHING AND INCIDENTALS

I covered these earlier in this chapter, on page 77. I suggest you go back and reread this section.

FLIES

See "A Beginning Selection of Flies" in Chapter 8, on page 60, "Flies for Trout Lakes."

KNOTS

11

Fly fishers' knots pose a brief challenge to the beginner; then they are all but forgotten and used automatically. There are only a few you'll need, but you'll definitely need those few. The best news is, *everyone* gets them eventually. If new to fishing knots, you'll soon discover that gaining control of all those ends and loops and twists makes nearly *anything* permissible— pinching more than one part of a knot between the same thumb and finger and squeezing parts between two *fingers* are common practice; some even clamp leader-ends in *teeth*. Tug and knead all knots until they are thoroughly snug, then trim them closely, leaving only a very short end.

IMPROVED CLINCH AND SKIP'S CLINCH

These are simple. The improved clinch is the well-known and now-standard version of the clinch, but it's come back as a tiny squiggle of leader—without fly or fish—a few critical times for me, so I worked out my own variation. Logic would call this new variation the "improved improved clinch"; taste wouldn't. So I gave it my name, in part because name-familiarity is akin to survival for those of us making a living in this odd little business of fly fishing.

After devoting far less than exhaustive research to the matter, I can say with absolute uncertainty that no one else has ever taken credit for inventing my simple knot and that it has never before appeared in print.

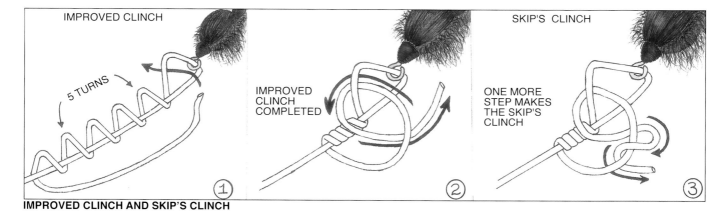

IMPROVED CLINCH AND SKIP'S CLINCH

DUNCAN LOOP

With sunken flies, the Duncan loop makes sense. It lets the fly swivel freely on a tiny loop of leader. But in practice, Brian has seldom found it more productive than the clinches. He now uses the Duncan loop only with bead-head imitations of leeches and chironomid pupae and with any large head-weighted fly with the potential for lots of head-dipping.

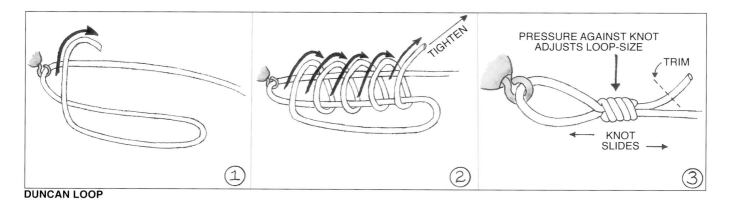

DUNCAN LOOP

DOUBLE SURGEON'S KNOT

This is an easy, sound knot for attaching a tippet to a leader. But some anglers still prefer the blood knot that follows.

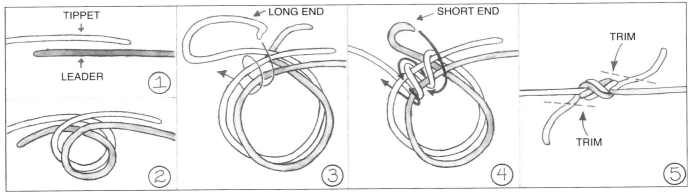

DOUBLE SURGEON'S KNOT

BLOOD KNOT

Brian and I generally use this knot for attaching the butt of a leader to the fairly permanent stretch of heavy, level monofilament we attach to the fly line. This level strand is, like many of our choices, a reflection of our elemental laziness—it allows us to attach new leaders with a blood knot, which we find easier to tie than the nail knot we'd have to tie if going straight to the fly line. (The nail knot follows.)

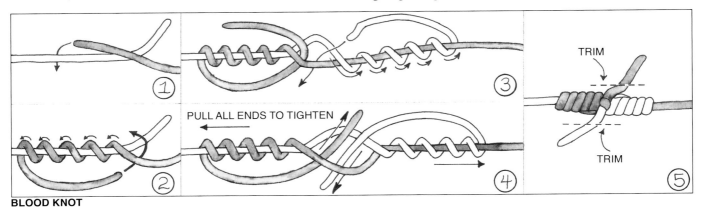

BLOOD KNOT

NAIL KNOT

The nail knot is the standard for attaching the heavy butt of a leader (or a short length of heavy level monofilament) to the tip of a fly line. Brian and I also use it to attach fly-line butts to backing.

To create a smooth transition from leader to fly line, so that the juncture of the two will slip easily through the rod's guides, Brian runs the butt of the leader up through the core of the line before making the nail knot, then coats the knot and line-tip with Pliobond (a general-purpose flexible glue) as shown below. But most fly fishers simply make and leave a bare nail knot at the tip of the line.

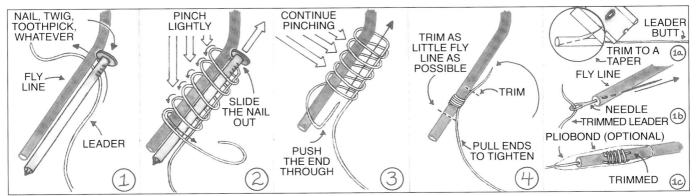

NAIL KNOT

BACKING TO REEL

The simple backing-to-reel knot performs exactly the duty that its name suggests, and it is the only knot you need for job.

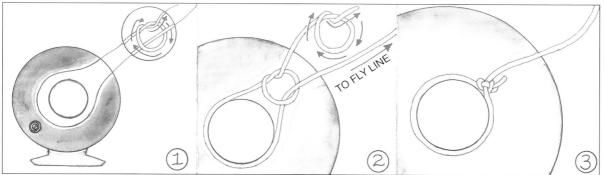

BACKING TO REEL

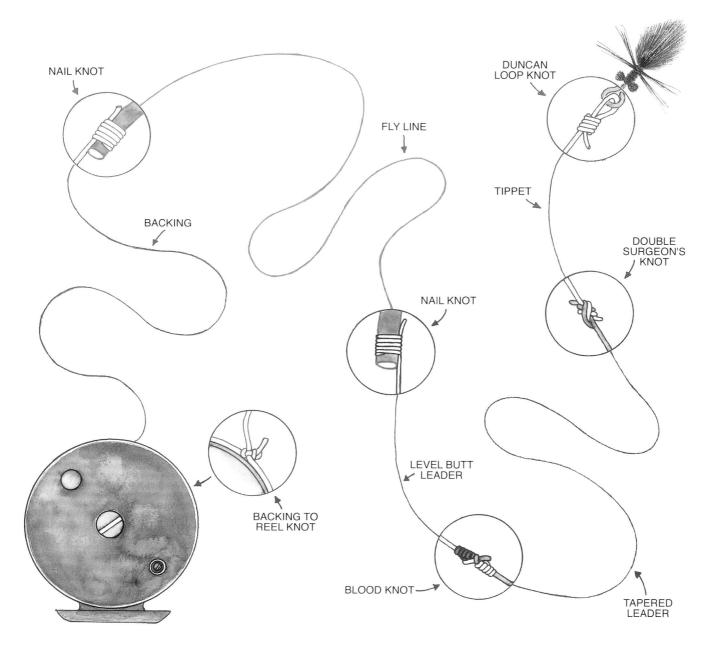

NAIL KNOT

BACKING

FLY LINE

NAIL KNOT

BACKING TO
REEL KNOT

LEVEL BUTT
LEADER

BLOOD KNOT

DUNCAN
LOOP KNOT

TIPPET

DOUBLE
SURGEON'S
KNOT

TAPERED
LEADER

I write this at the end of a day of fishing an Idaho river in which the brown trout generally fought harder, leaped higher, and leaped more often than the rainbows. According to what I've written below, that's not right—the brown is supposed to be a subdued fighter while the rainbow's fight should be spectacular. Clearly, trout are not easily characterized. Bear that in mind as you read the descriptions to come.

Bear in mind, too, that there are other, less-common, trouts and troutlike fishes that live in lakes and provide fine sport for the fly fisher: the Atlantic salmon, rainbow-cutthroat hybrid, and grayling to name but a few.

RAINBOW TROUT

Though once confined to a slim strip of North America's west coast, the rainbow, due to his easy adjustment to hatchery life, is likely now the most common lake-dwelling trout in the entire continent. He is known as a wild fighter and free leaper, and he is second only to the brown as an intelligent, difficult trout—but a well-fed, angler-wise rainbow can be as elusive as any brown.

Bright as polished silver, the rainbow got his name from the red or pink band running down each flank.

BROWN TROUT

The brown trout was transplanted from Europe to America more than one hundred years ago. General opinion holds that the brown's plodding struggle on the line falls well short of the rainbow's brilliant athletics. But opinion also holds that the brown is inherently the brightest of the trouts—even when hungry and unfamiliar with the fly fisher's chicanery he is no fool.

As his name suggests, the brown trout is overall brownish to tannish with a sort of yellow on the belly and sometimes along the sides. He is heavily spotted, with most spots black, some red.

EASTERN BROOK TROUT

Not quite a trout, the brook trout is a troutlike "char." Eastern North America was once his range, but he now reproduces across the continent. He is, in fact, so good at reproducing that he may overpopulate and stunt. Generally no great fighter or thinker (though Brian has found him a sporadic and therefore *bewildering* feeder), the brook trout is lovely and easy to love.

His colors are striking (downright *sensational* at spawning time): green back with vermiculation, side-spots of yellow and red, white-tipped lower fins.

CUTTHROAT TROUT

The cutthroat is native to western North America and seems determined to remain at home by faring poorly in hatcheries and outside his original range. He is comparable to the brook trout in gullibility and fight.

The various subspecies of cutthroats vary widely in appearance. Usually there is some heavy spotting and at least some yellow along the sides. The closest thing to a sure sign is the slash of red beneath each jaw line, though even that is sometimes faint.

FIRST LAKE, NEW LAKE

SKIP MORRIS

A beginner's first trout lake, or a new lake to an experienced fly fisher, is a puzzle to be solved. Of course, the solution can never be complete—the secrets and moods and nuances of even a single trout lake are so copious and complex that no one is ever likely to understand them all. But I am talking here about solving only enough of the puzzle so that the fly fisher finds and catches a decent number of trout. When the fly fisher fails to solve enough of the puzzle, it is usually due to one, or more, of these four reasons:

1. a lack of confidence

2. poor observation

3. rigid thinking

4. the puzzle is pretty much unsolvable

The following describes how to deal effectively with each of these reasons for failure.

A lack of confidence: The experienced angler comes to a new lake armed with confidence born of past successes. The neophyte lake-fisher comes to his first lake only with doubts. If you are the latter, I suggest you simply proceed as though you had confidence, and trust in yourself and what you've learned from this book. The more you fish trout lakes, the more confident you'll grow, and the more these words and pictures will spill out into the reality of your fishing.

Poor observation: Good fly fishers are observant—there are no good *un*observant fly fishers. But if you are not yet a good fly fisher, remember that slim experience can often be fully compensated for by a keen eye. Watch everything that might even possibly have meaning—the water, the insects, the birds, the trout, even other anglers. Look for signs, clues. Be alert. Observe.

Rigid thinking: Rigid thinking is a kind of mental blindness that spreads to the eyes. The result is that both mind and eye are indifferent—for the fly fisher it is a disastrous combination. Rigid thinking, in fly fishing lakes, is persisting with damselfly-nymph imitations around the reeds for an hour and a half without a touch because someone said or wrote that it is damselfly-time. Flexible thinking is fishing the damsel without a touch for only twenty minutes, then trying an entirely different type or stretch of shoreline, then trying a different depth or fly or approach until something works. Good fly fishers are flexible thinkers.

The problem is pretty much unsolvable: This last matter, that lake-trout sometimes cannot be caught—that is, beyond the occasional suicidal rebel—is simply a reality you must accept. Trout sometimes stop feeding—how can you get such fish to take a fly? Other times, trout are feeding on things too small for a fly to imitate, such as zooplankton or "*Daphnia*," a speck-size water flea. And there are other reasons lake-trout can't be caught, many of which no one seems to understand. The point is, even the keenest lake fishers fail—I've even seen Brian, my co-author, fail, and he's a lake fisher of the first order. So don't take it all too seriously; if fishing is now slow, an hour or two later it may be fast.

NEW LAKE

To the challenge of an unfamiliar trout lake, a seasoned fly fisher brings experience, a keen eye, and a willingness to experiment. His approach is usually a loose progression of logical steps, but nearly always there are surprises. Following is a description of a seasoned fly fisher's first day on a new trout lake, with you cast in the fly fisher's role. The beginner would be wise to read it carefully, so that on a real lake, he may repeat the role with conviction.

Soft-blue sky drapes itself everywhere this spring morning and, to your left, a soft-yellow sun gently casts its color from just above distant tree tops. The now and then light breezes find only an occasional cottony cloud to coax across the sun, momentarily turning off the slow build of the day's heat. You stand at the lake's edge. You struggle to bring sharp consciousness up through the languor of the morning's spell. You scan the surface—no fly fisher can come to new water and resist playing over it with the imagination. This lake is full of promise, as new water seems always to be, and you feel as though every likely stretch of shoreline and every bay and all the unseen shoals must be swarming with careless three-pounders. You remind yourself that it's never quite that easy and good, and seldom even close—fishing will likely be at least something of a challenge, and the three-pounders, if you find any, will likely be surprises.

You look to the lake-side trees and grasses and brush and inspect them for caddisfly or mayfly adults, for flying ants, or whatever you can find. You shake a few branches and sweep your hand through the grasses to see what flies. A few caddisflies flutter away, and you find a couple of *Callibaetis* mayflies. You inspect the rocks and dirt and gravel. There is a dry pale dragonfly shuck on a watermelon-size rock, just up from the water. You inspect the shallow reeds and find, among the many that are bare, a few that carry each a ragged whitened damselfly-shuck up their stalk, and wave it about with every puff of wind.

Now you lower your head close to the water and observe. A couple of scuds swim in steady straight paths just above the gravel bottom. Nothing else shows, so you pick up a hand-size rock. Suctioned to its underside you find two leeches, one dark-olive with black spots, the other tan. When you first moved the rock, a big dragonfly nymph darted swiftly away.

Now you sweep your gaze out over lake's surface again, but this time with purpose. To your left, rimmed with yellow haze, are a pair of dark anglers in dark float tubes, occasionally turning to flash their orange backrests. A lone angler in an aluminum pram is straight out near the far shore. No one seems to have a fish on . . . then you notice a solitary rise, well out and to your right. You wait, hoping that it is only one in a string of rises, but no others appear. Still, it could mean something later.

You see a fish jump, just out from a cluster of logs against the shore and well up to your left. Again you watch and hope that it tells of surface feeders, but, like the rise, it is solitary and probably unimportant. So you store it in memory and continue. You look for swooping birds. There are none. You look for bays and points and logs and reeds and lily pads and then you look at the slope of the shoreline around the lake and imagine how it continues into the water. Then you begin to put up a rod.

You remember all that you've seen as you row away from shore, though you could just as likely be in a float tube, pumping away with swim fins. You have three rods with you: one with a floating line and an imitation mayfly emerger, one with a type I line and an imitation damselfly nymph, and one with a type III line and a big nymph. The flies on the first two rods are mainly there to keep the rods' tips safely tethered, but the particular fly patterns are just best guesses—it's about time for the *Callibaetis* mayflies, and the salesman at the fly shop yesterday had told you that the damselflies were just starting to show in the local lakes. (You bought a couple of leaders from him as thanks for the information.) The fly on the third rod is the one you plan to start with.

You do so by making a cast, and then stripping line from the reel as you feed the line out with shakes of the rod, then rowing a ways to take up the slack, stripping and shaking out more line, rowing again, and repeating this process until most or all of the line is out. Now you troll, a lazy, varied tempo with the oars, working the fly up and down, side to side, slowly and quickly, and all that's between.

You turn on your fish finder. As you row, you watch its screen for trout and depth and contour, you watch the water for insects or their leftover shucks, you watch the shoreline for signs of trout and the sky for birds. You have forgotten all about the rod when finally it jumps.

The reel screeches and you snatch up the rod to feel live resistance. Minutes later a 16-inch rainbow trout lies in your net. You cradle the fish gently and, knowing that you could easily kill it by performing the next task incorrectly, carefully use a throat pump to remove the remains of its last few swallows from the base of its throat. Those remains include a large scud, three small chironomid pupae (two of which are still squirming), a damselfly nymph, and some tiny specs that are *Daphnia*. An open-minded feeder, you think. But the three chironomids suggest a theme, especially the two that were taken so recently that they are still alive.

That's when you start to see chironomid shucks on the surface. A couple of adults fly by, rising slowly through the air. Then you see a chironomid struggling from its shuck and finally flying off. No trout rise, but this holds promise. You row about, looking for the heaviest insect-concentration; you watch the fish finder for trout and depth. You row across and upwind of the heaviest part of the hatch, quietly lower an anchor off the bow, and then lower one off the stern. The size of the chironomids you took from the trout matches the size of the floating shucks, so you loosely assume that your sample-chironomids and those that are hatching are all of a kind. The ones from the trout's throat are brown. To the end of the floating line you tie a long leader, four feet of tippet, and a brown chironomid pupa that matches the size of the natural. After casting the whole thing across wind, you let the wind work the line down, and then you retrieve it with almost absurd slowness. Ten minutes later, two times through the process, your line pulls and you set the hook; a half-moment later a fair-size trout flies from the water and shivers back down in a splash. In the next 45 minutes you hook five more trout and land three. Then the strikes stop, but you can see that the chironomids are still coming off. You add a strike indicator to your leader, four feet from the fly, and cast again. Because the last trout took your fly as it was first sinking, you suspect that the trout had moved up, taking the pupae nearer the surface. You are right, and you land three more trout before the hatch dies.

This is a place for chironomids. You make a mental note of it, or maybe you even write it in a notebook, then it's back to trolling, and observing.

Over the next half an hour you have but one strike which became a few throbs down the rod and then nothing. But something just splashed by those floating logs near shore; then you see a quiet rise there. You remember the trout that jumped near shoreline logs when you first arrived. This is worth looking into.

You reel in some of the line you had put out for trolling, then shoot the remainder in close among the logs and let it sink a bit. After three casts you hook a modest trout. After five more casts, another. After ten more casts, nothing. A few active fish poking around the edges, you think, but nothing more.

So you return to trolling out from the lake's edge, watching everything. Forty-five minutes later, you have landed one more modest trout. The day has been warming steadily—two hours ago you pulled off the light jacket; an hour ago you began perspiring under your hat—then a high cloud-layer kindly crept over to cool the air. Hunger makes you glance at your watch—11:50 seems a good excuse for lunch. But you should have eaten as you trolled, because you see, back where you have just come from, swallows gliding busily over the water. You forget about lunch and hurry to them.

With the swallows you expect insects and you find them—dark little *Callibaetis* mayfly duns stand on the water with abdomens and heads and wings stretched upwards, as though standing on their tiptoes. The cloud layer encouraged them to hatch. You scoop one up in your aquarium net, pinch it lightly by the wings and turn it over. Its underside is olive-gray and its size corresponds with a size-14 hook. No surprises here. You pick up the rod with the floating line and tie the mayfly emerger on again, the very fly that started the day with this line; then you lightly rub the fly with fly floatant and smear some thinly along the leader and tippet.

On your right, a trout snaps up a mayfly with a splash; on your left, another takes a mayfly in a solemn sip. You watch for a pattern to the trout's feeding, a series of rises, but there is no pattern. The mayflies aren't so plentiful that the trout can path-rise—they must take them as they find them. So you put your fly between two simultaneous rises, hoping that at least one of the trout will wander close enough to find it. One does, and a nose drops gently over the fly.

For almost an hour, the fishing is active and steady. Then the rises lessen as the hatch increases. You try swimming a nymph slowly near the bottom on a type II line. The action returns.

Then the clouds break up and the sun-shy mayflies halt their hatching.

You troll back towards the boat launch. You lazily row as, finally, you eat your lunch. Then you hook two fish in quick succession, so you troll back through there again and hook another. Nothing comes on your third try, but this spot is worth remembering. You continue on to land where you launched, and find a cool place in the shade and nap.

The whine of mosquitoes around your face awakens you in late afternoon. The sun is still out, but the air is cooling. Shadows are long and the lake is barely ruffled from the occasional light breeze. You shake the sleep from your brain and stretch it from your body. Soon you are again trolling up the now slightly familiar left side of the lake.

You stop, a few strikes and slightly fewer landed fish later, where the mayflies were hatching earlier. You drop both anchors and check the depth on your fish finder. It is 15 feet deep. You decide on the rod with the type II line, but can't decide what fly to put up. The big nymph has worked well trolled, but you feel like trying something else. An imitation scud makes sense, since there are always scuds. But there are always leeches too, and you wonder if a big leech might attract a big trout, so you tie a big imitation leech to your tippet. You can always go back to the big nymph or a scud later.

You cast out line and fly, count the sinking of the line—"one one-thousand, two one-thousand, three . . . "—then begin a slow retrieve. Your fourth cast—you've worked your count up to 12—puts a shred of green plant on the hook—the fly is scraping the bottom. You back up to a count of 10. On the sixth cast, just when you were about to change to the big nymph, you connect with a good trout.

You try the other side of the boat and eventually hook a small trout. Then you go back to the big nymph and fishing seems to pick up.

By sunset, you have moved the boat and reset the anchors several times, steadily working back to the boat launch. Fishing has been fair, but steady, and one big fish had your backing well out without a sign of slowing and you uttering a surprised "Good Lord" when the hook came free.

For the past half hour you've been seeing occasional rises. The lake is flat, and you think you've been seeing more rising down past your launch point. You arrive there to find trout rising in good numbers. You watch one rise, you wait, but no second rise follows. You watch another. As its rings die, a second rise forms only about three feet away from the first. As that rise dies, another forms—this trout is path-rising.

You put up a chironomid-emerger imitation on your floating line. Ten minutes later, you feel certain that your fly was in place for two rising trout, yet the fish only skipped a sequential rise when they came to it. You haven't been observant, but now that changes. You peer about the surface looking for evidence. A tiny chironomid shuck appears; an imitation will be about three hook-sizes smaller than the fly you've been fishing. You switch to a size-18 imitation emerger, spend a few tries to put it in a rise-path, and hook a trout. The trout take this fly consistently—that is, when you can get it quietly into a rise-path. As the last edge of the sun drops behind the hills, you trade your polarized glasses for a pair with clear glass.

At last the light fades into near-blackness; the rises become numerous and calm. You make your casts to the elongated gleam of moonlight on the water—the only place you can hope to see your fly. You hook two more trout this way; the best is almost your three-pounder. And as you row back to the boat launch, you think how unlikely it seems that beneath such a small and quiet rise lay your best fish of the day.

This is a good day's lake fishing—about three dozen trout landed, more hooked. It is also a long day; most anglers would have fished only a few hours—a morning or an afternoon, or both with a long break between.

And things don't always go this smoothly. Brian and I have fished together when the catching was hot for only half an hour, then not a touch the rest of the day. Other times, the fishing's been fast for as long as three hours, with good fishing before and after.

In the six weeks one spring that I and my wife, Carol, lived near Big and Little Lac Le Jeune in British Columbia, we had many days of the same hot, then spotty, then steady fishing described in this typical day. Usually, we found fish if we were willing to move and experiment whenever the activity died. But even there, as familiar as we had become with the two lakes, there were days when catching a trout seemed impossible, and other days when the only real fishing came and left in a flurry (and, of course, days when all the trout in one lake or the other seemed bent upon taking our flies from morning till dark). But this was no surprise to me—I've seen the same kind of unpredictable and erratic fishing on my local lakes for decades. And I've seen it on trout streams just as often.

The point is, fishing is always in flux. And though it tends loosely to follow a path composed of certain principles and schedules, it often wanders off on a whim. When it does, even the experienced lake fisher with both feet firmly planted on that path may have nothing to show for it. This is when the angler must try something different, perhaps something even unlikely, if he is to catch trout when the rules seem not to apply. Fishing a deep nymph when mayflies are popping off the surface, presenting a big imitation leech to trout that seem to be on chironomids, or casting to the shoreline in a lake renowned for its productive shoals—all these may seem like desperate acts, but when experience fails, keen fly fishers will turn to the wildest experimentation. And often enough, it works.

Of course, often it doesn't. As I said earlier, sometimes lake-trout, like stream-trout, simply can't be caught. The angler may practice casting, eat, admire the lovely place he has chosen for this day (with few exceptions, trout lakes *are* lovely), pull up a few water plants or poke around in the shallows after insects to study, take a break and try again later, or pack up and leave. What he can't do is catch enough trout to be worth the required effort.

Sometimes, one or two anglers may have good fishing while another couple of dozen catch very little or nothing. The difference may be observation or it may be experience or it may be that the one or two stumbled upon a solution or it may be that the one or two know that particular lake intimately. There's a lot to be said for simply knowing well a particular lake, and I've said it in another chapter in this book—"On Knowing a Lake," which begins on the next page—so I won't repeat it here.

As they are in streams, trout in lakes can be easy to catch or confoundingly difficult or somewhere in between.

I've talked a lot here about the difficulties of trout-lake fishing. If I've given the impression that it is a solemn business requiring constant precision and extensive knowledge, then I've gone way too far. Fly fishing trout lakes is supposed to be fun, and on a lake with a good stock of trout, even the novice will likely catch a few.

On the other hand, imagine what can be done with a *real* understanding of fly fishing and trout lakes. You begin to see the possibilities.

14

ON KNOWING A LAKE

Allll lakes and all the trout and creatures within lakes are governed by one universal set of principles and factors, and yet each lake is unique. Oxygen, temperature, water clarity, depth, plant growth, and a hundred other elements find a different balance in each lake; as a result, each lake takes on its own character.

Essentially, lakes are at once both as uniform and as singular as people.

Therefore, to really learn one trout lake is to gain insight into all trout lakes, though each lake presents a new challenge.

So I suggest that you return to a particular lake enough times that you develop some intimacy with it. What you will learn from trolling along the same drop-off or meeting a mayfly hatch over the same shoal again and again will refine skills and insight that will be invaluable on other lakes. Nevertheless, be flexible and always aware that no two lakes, however near or far from one another, are the same.

Bear all this in mind as we examine three fine trout lakes. Look for similarities, and for differences.

LAC LE JEUNE

Actually, there are *two* lakes in the Kamloops region of Canada's British Columbia that share this name, and through a small, lazy, very short connecting stream, the same clear water. Big Lac Le Jeune, two broad miles of mainly deep water (up to nearly 80 feet deep) that can quickly turn from playtime blue to solemn gray whenever a dark cloud slips over, is a bent arm whose shoulder has been replaced with the small, shallow (no deeper than

BIG LAC LE JEUNE

35 feet), friendly oval that is Little Lac Le Jeune. The trout of both lakes are the free-leaping Kamloops rainbow.

For more than a dozen weeks spread over three consecutive years I lived on or near the shores of these lakes, and therefore feel I have developed some understanding of each. But fly-fishing guide Gordon Honey has been fishing these lakes for decades and living on them year round for the past five years. He knows them better than perhaps anyone—which is precisely why I relied heavily on his knowledge of them to supplement my own.

Consider as you read on how different (and, predictably, how similar) two lakes not only near one another but sharing the very same water can be.

Both Big and Little Lac Le Jeune have only modest daytime hatches of chironomids, though Gordon suspects good evening hatches on the little lake. Both lakes are heavy with scuds and contain good numbers of leeches. Dry-fly fishing can be excellent on either lake—on the big lake such fishing is usually best during hatches of mayfly and caddis, while on the little lake it is caddis, or sometimes hatching or egg-laying chironomids at dusk, that draw trout to the surface. And that's about where the main similarities end.

LITTLE LAC LE JEUNE

Big Lac Le Jeune is among the earliest and best *Callibaetis* mayfly lakes in the Kamloops Region. But Little Lac Le Jeune has very few mayflies—seldom is their hatching sufficient to move the trout. The big lake contains only modest numbers of damselfly and dragonfly with their hatches only occasionally good, and always spotty. In sharp contrast the little lake is a great producer of the dragonfly (which few lakes are) and its numbers of damselflies in a good year are staggering. Both lakes contain ample small caddis, but only the big lake has sufficient numbers of big travelling-sedge caddis, which come off here mainly at night, to produce good fishing.

Additionally, the better trout of the big lake seldom move to a dry fly without the added attraction of a good hatch as the main draw. But the ample reel-screeching trout of the little lake are willing to come to a floating fly from fairly deep often enough without a hatch that it is always worth showing them one on speculation.

Further, the little lake usually comes on in spring several weeks before the big lake. And Gordon and I can tell you with the certainty of experience that often as not, one of the two lakes is generous with its fish while the other is miserly, and the roles can reverse on any week, any day, any hour.

HENRY'S LAKE, IDAHO

Lying shallow and broad (about five miles across) in a valley between two crinkled mountain rows, Henry's Lake melds with its valley to a flatness that seems, somehow, to invite the explosive winds that can so suddenly arise to rush across them. There are really big trout in this tinged-green water; a four- or even five-pounder is no event—that requires a trout of at least seven pounds. The trout are mostly cutthroat, with lesser numbers of brook trout and cutthroat-rainbow hybrids. So thick are water plants, hoisting their tips nearly to the surface, that most anglers limit themselves to fishing the few open areas around the lake's edges. Bill Schiess and a few other old hands on the lake have learned to penetrate the heavy growth with their flies in their search for the largest trout.

Bill is a guide whose specialty is the odd and exceptional Henry's Lake. Though my wife Carol and I lived on the lake for over a month one September and October in a comfortable cabin at Staley Springs Lodge and fished the lake a few times (the Henry's Fork of the Snake River, the Madison River, dozens of creeks and ponds and other lakes, and the vast opportunities of Yellowstone Park are all distractingly near, and drew us away often), Bill is the main source of the information here.

HENRY'S LAKE DURING A SPELL OF COLD WEATHER IN LATE SEPTEMBER

Henry's Lake is exceptionally rich and, consequently, heavy with creatures trout eat. The most abundant of these is the scud—here, it abounds. Chironomids are second in abundance and hatch in such profusion that Bill and his clients sometimes wear insect-masks to avoid inhaling the flying adults. Additionally, there are lots of *Callibaetis* mayflies and assorted caddis. Damselflies are cyclical: just modest hatches usually, but about every third year the sculling nymphs teem in their migration to the near-surface, then to shore.

Yet despite this wealth of insects of which so many are often lying helpless at the surface, Henry's almost utterly lacks good surface fishing. And seldom are its surface-feeding trout over eight inches long. As Bill says in one of his letters: "In 14 years of fishing the lake very seriously, I have only fished with dry flies three times." He adds that "even during the damselfly hatch we fish nymphs on the bottom." This is an anomaly, since a good damselfly hatch usually calls for the fly to be fished within three feet of the surface. Bill sums up the whole surface-fishing-on-Henrys Lake matter neatly: "We use sinking lines about 99% of the time."

In sharp contrast, my wife Carol, our friend Mike Seim, and I had a brilliant day of flipping nymphs to two-pound rainbows lying within a foot of the surface around the shallow edges of an air-clear lake not two dozen miles from Henry's.

COURTESY AND SAFETY

15

COURTESY

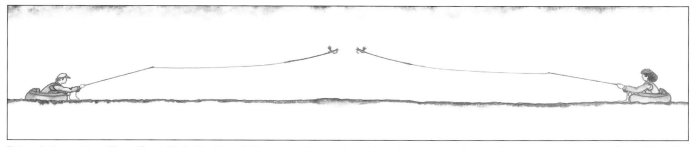

Brian follows the "Two-Cast Rule," which tells us to stay at least two long casts from other water-borne anglers. New fly fishers might make it the Three-Cast Rule to adjust for their green casting skills. (The quality of the caster's instruction comes into question somewhere around the Five-Cast Rule.)

Never force conversation on a stranger. He or she is probably there just to fish—and find solitude. If you ask a question or two and receive only answers—no questions or attempts to keep the conversation alive—gracefully follow the implied suggestion that you leave the angler alone.

Keep conversation with friends across the water to a minimum if other anglers are anywhere near. If you are sharing your boat with a partner, keep your voices down.

Quietly approach a promising area, to avoid alarming trout *and* other anglers. It's rude to storm in by power boat and set other watercraft rocking. Drop your speed while still well away, then kill the engine and row the last, say, 150 feet (unless you are using or have at hand a quiet electric outboard motor, but even then, proceed slowly).

Everything just said applies in reverse for leaving.

Use your power boat courteously and your fishing and popularity will surely improve.

SAFETY

Safety comes from preparation, knowledge, common sense, and the good sense to trust one's instincts.

Preparation: Maintain your watercraft; keep it in safe, dependable condition. Consider having one Coast Guard-approved life vest aboard *any* kind of watercraft (yes, even a float tube or kick-boat) for *every* occupant. Actually *wearing* said vest (or vests) is even safer than simply having one at hand—when in the slightest doubt, don a vest. (See "Life Vest" in Chapter 10, "Boats, Float Tubes, and Tackle," on page 71.) Keeping a small first-aid kit aboard is also prudent.

Knowledge: Know your watercraft. Information on its safe use should come with it, may even be printed on it. Find that information, read it, take it seriously. The Coast Guard can provide pamphlets, and courses in some places, on the rules and principles of safely operating a boat (much of this information also pertains to float tubes and other watercraft). While the Coast Guard's jurisdiction includes waters used for commercial transport (which includes some lakes, usually big ones), lakes used solely for recreation (recreational fishing, for example) are under the jurisdiction of the local sheriff's department, which can also provide information.

Know *yourself*, too—how well can you swim? how experienced are you with water and watercraft? Know your personal limitations and stay well within them.

Common Sense: An angler in a float tube is far slower, far smaller, and far more difficult to see than an angler in a 12-foot boat—this float-tube angler is also in peril if that boat is equipped with an outboard motor and is coming too near. Let us hope that the angler in the boat is responsible, watchful, and sober, which usually he is . . . but sometimes is not. If not, then the angler in the boat is in danger himself because with the thrust and speed of an outboard come a whole new set of risks—collisions with snags, floating debris, shallow shoals that extend far out, and other morons with outboards.

All of this is common sense, and if everyone who set out on water trusted in common sense, far fewer would come to trouble than now do.

The Good Sense to Trust One's Instincts: Man's arrogance tells him to ignore his feelings and trust only his wonderful intellect. This can lead to trouble: Instincts serve a purpose—mainly survival—and serve it well, while intellect can lose itself in theories and details and miss what's important. Besides, intellect isn't all that consistent and consequently not all that dependably wonderful. When a wind-torn lake looks dark and dangerous, when early spring water seems eager to push its icy chill through your light waders into your bones, when any aspect of fishing lakes erects the hairs on your arms and neck or just feels threatening or wrong, have the good sense to heed and trust your instincts.

Devote some time to safety; even a little helps. It's the best and cheapest insurance around.